The Four Traits
of a Cherished Muslimah

WORKBOOK

First published in the UK by Beacon Books and Media Ltd
103 Washway Rd, Cheshire, Sale M33 7TY

Copyright © Sara Malik 2020

The right of Sara Malik to be identified as the author of this work has been asserted in accordance with the Copyright, Designs and Patents Act 1988. All rights reserved. This book may not be reproduced, scanned, transmitted or distributed in any printed or electronic form or by any means without the prior written permission from the copyright owner, except in the case of brief quotations embedded in critical reviews and other non-commercial uses permitted by copyright law.

First paperback edition published in 2020

www.beaconbooks.net

ISBN: 978-1-912356-33-1 Paperback
ISBN: 978-1-912356-34-8 eBook
ISBN: 978-1-912356-35-5 Workbook
ISBN: 978-1-912356-36-2 eWorkbook

Cataloging-in-Publication record for this book is available from the British Library

Illustrations by Elliot Flynn

The Four Traits
of a Cherished Muslimah

WORKBOOK

Sara Malik

*He gives wisdom to whom He wills,
and whoever has been given wisdom has certainly been given much good.*

Al-Baqarah (2:269)

Dedication

To all women who want to do something different and make a difference,

who are not satisfied with the mediocre and believe they are powerful beyond measure:

I believe that you, too, can be a mercy to the world.

May we be with the Messenger of Allah ﷺ.

Contents

Gratitude	vii
Welcome	1
Introduction	3
Foundations	19
1. Purpose	21
2. Balance	36
3. Gratitude	45
4. Self-Care	56
5. Communication	61
6. Respecting Others	79
Nourishment	91
7. Guardianship	95
8. Giving Love	107
9. Healing	113
10. Time	124
11. Self-Respect	133
12. Self-Discipline	143
A Garden with Flowers	155
The 99 Names of Allah	157
Endnotes	163
Bibliography	165

Gratitude

I am so thankful to Allah that He blessed me with the desire to change whenever things could be better, and to seek help from 'those who knew' when I needed help. I thank Him for giving me the ability to train and learn skills that have helped me to improve my own life, and in turn, the resources and capacity to be able to use these skills to benefit others. And I thank Allah for Beacon Books, who used their skills to publish this workbook so that many women can 'be the change they want to see in the world'.

I praise Him and beg Him to guide me towards His light, and I am so thankful to Him for leading me to my treasured teacher, Shaykh Mohammed Faid Said, where my heart and questions finally found peace and rest. May Allah protect him and preserve him, and allow us to benefit from him, Ameen! I thank Allah for my teacher Shaykh Sulayman Van Ael, who taught me and connected me with the 99 names of Allah through his love and awe for the King of Kings. May Allah reward him with Jannah, 'and more'.

And most importantly, I thank Allah for my loving and supportive husband, Jawad. As our young daughter says, you are the definition of a gentleman. For all of our talks over breakfast, dinner, tea and great coffee, for all of the times 'we need to talk', for all of the loving times and exasperating times, for all of the love and tears, here's to the next part of our adventure... may we draw closer to Rasulullah ﷺ with every utterance of 'La ilāha il-Allah' and every completion of 'Muhammad ur-Rasulullah' in every glance and breath, as many times as is encompassed by the knowledge of Allah.

Welcome

I am delighted for you to be reading *The Four Traits of a Cherished Muslimah Workbook*, the companion to my book *The Four Traits of a Cherished Muslimah*. Simply taking the time out to read this workbook shows that you are already taking brave steps towards improving your marriage, and I congratulate you for your dedication! InshaAllah, you will learn techniques to strengthen your relationship with your husband, and I pray that this book helps you and transforms your life. Ameen!

Let's start with Bismillah! This workbook has been written so that the skills within it can be implemented gradually, which, if done effectively, can allow you to develop habits that last a lifetime. Try not to rush the process or you may find yourself disappointed with the results, and find that you miss valuable moments of realisation, which in themselves can be life-changing.

There are two parts to this book: Foundations and Nourishment, and in both parts, you will learn how to cultivate specific habits for each of the four traits. First, you will learn about the foundation or core habits to develop, and then you will add more habits which will, InshaAllah, nourish you and your marriage. It's a gradual and incremental procedure: you apply these habits in your life systematically and chronologically, just like you learnt everything gradually when you were very young. First you learnt to crawl, then stand, and then climb! As a general guide, I would recommend sticking to learning and reflecting on one new habit per week, building up these habits as the weeks progress. In total there are 12 habits, so if you can dedicate 12 weeks to this journey, then I am confident that you will find the process transformative.

Over the last decade, I have personally worked through each of the exercises included in this book, and I hope you can reap as many benefits from these mentoring exercises as I did. It is my desire that your life is transformed by letting go of old ideas, attitudes and habits that hinder your marriage and may not be useful anymore. The exercises in this book will take you through a process of finding out who you really are. Like an onion, when you peel away each layer, you find a new, more authentic version of yourself. Complete the ones that you are drawn to; flexibility is the key. Be patient, and don't let your old attitudes pull you away from your inner, feminine essence that is waiting to be discovered. I have included examples, where applicable, which have been taken from the ladies I coach, modifying them slightly to make them suited to the context of the exercises.

Even though I love structure, there is *no perfect template for marriage*. I believe that 'good enough' is simply good enough! All marriages have their ups and downs; all couples argue and face issues—mine included! Marriage is about two people living together and communicating. If we are successful in getting out exactly what is inside us, we feel 'understood', 'heard' and 'seen'. Let's work toward understanding, hearing and seeing the people in our lives!

I'm not saying this is the only way. There are many ways to arrive at the same destination, and I have found this way of inner belief and unconditional respect highly successful, both in my own marriage and when I coach other women. Just allow yourself to play with the concepts in this book and see where they take you. This is not an imposition or a set of rules; it is another choice, one which worked amazingly well for me, Alhamdulillah.

Be gentle with yourself! As you start this workbook and begin learning new ways of being and giving up unhealthy patterns of behaviour, you might start feeling a bit guilty about the current state of your marriage. Just take heart in the knowledge that when you change, Allah changes your condition.

Verily, Allah will not change the condition of a people until they change what is in themselves.

Ar-Ra'ad (13:11)

As humans, we are extremely powerful beings. Not only do we have the power to destroy our fellow men/women's confidence and well-being, but we also have the power to bring out the very best in them. Becoming aware of this power—which is wisdom—will encourage you to move from a place of control to a place of quiet and serenity.

This workbook has been designed to be completed while reading or having read *The Four Traits of a Cherished Muslimah*, and for each habit you will be told which parts of the book the worksheets correspond to (indicated by 'Recommended Reading Points'). So grab a pen and a cup of tea or coffee, and let's go!

Introduction

Recommended Reading Point: The Four Traits of a Cherished Muslimah:
Preface & Introduction

This chapter focuses on your inner garden and where it needs to be cultivated and nourished. You will take an initial stock-check of your four traits, and see which ones you need to improve. You will also take a look at what's working in your life, and what is not.

Why read this book?

In *The Four Traits of a Cherished Muslimah*, women learn how to nourish their marriages by manifesting their innate traits of leadership, love, wisdom and justice. The premise of the book is clearcut: it takes more than just love to nourish one's marriage. When I told one of my friends that this was the subtitle of my book, she joked, 'Yes, it takes blood and sweat, too!' Jokes aside, a nourished marriage requires a lot of flexibility, wisdom, respect and boundaries, as well as lots of love.

Exercise 0.1

Before you continue, pause for a moment and reflect on why you have actually made the decision to read this book. What is important to you about marriage? There are so many books published on marriage, so why read this one? Which other books have you read? What did you find useful/not useful?

The Inner Garden

The only world that's true is simply
In the garden of your mind
Water daily what you plant there
And it seems that soon you'll find

Many flowers, herbs and fruits
And vegetables and roots as well
Growing slowly, healthily,
Organic seeds will start to swell

Natural rain will grace the greens
And butterflies will drink the dew
Flowers will begin to poke their tendrils
Towards the sky of blue

Keep the mind all free of clutter,
Memories past best left behind
Tend your garden, pluck the weeds,
A Heaven's gate is so sublime

Every day you must remember,
Discipline will clear the path
Promptly you'll see robins, warblers,
Sparrows, bluebirds in the bath

The bubbling granite fountain is placed
Squarely in the center so
That you can sit back gracefully, and
Gently watch your garden grow

Sally Shields - Gently Watch Your Garden Grow

Exercise 0.2 My Inner Garden Metaphors

Recommended Reading Point: The Four Traits of a Cherished Muslimah: The Inner Garden (page 2)

The metaphor of the inner garden helps ladies to visualise clearing, growth, nourishment, relating to others and setting boundaries. Think of your life as a garden, and on the following page, describe what your inner garden was like in the past, what it is like right now, in the present (what it looks like, how it feels, what sort of things you have in there, what you like to do there, etc.) and how you would like it to be in the future. Go into as much detail as possible—this is a chance to be creative and let your unconscious bring out as much detail as it wants. If you don't feel that creative, think of this exercise in terms of your life: where you were in the past, where you are now and where you would like to be in the future.

MY INNER GARDEN IN THE PAST

MY INNER GARDEN IN THE PRESENT

MY INNER GARDEN IN THE FUTURE

The Four Traits of a Cherished Muslimah Workbook

Exercise 0.3 The 4 Traits

Recommended Reading Point: The Four Traits of a Cherished Muslimah: The Four Traits (page 9)

The four traits of a Cherished Muslimah are leadership, love, wisdom and justice. We all have these traits within us and manifest them in some form or another. Read through the characteristics of the four traits in *The Four Traits of a Cherished Muslimah*, and reflect upon which traits you typically manifest or are the most familiar to you. Do you tend to manifest certain traits more than others, or resonate more with a particular one, or two?

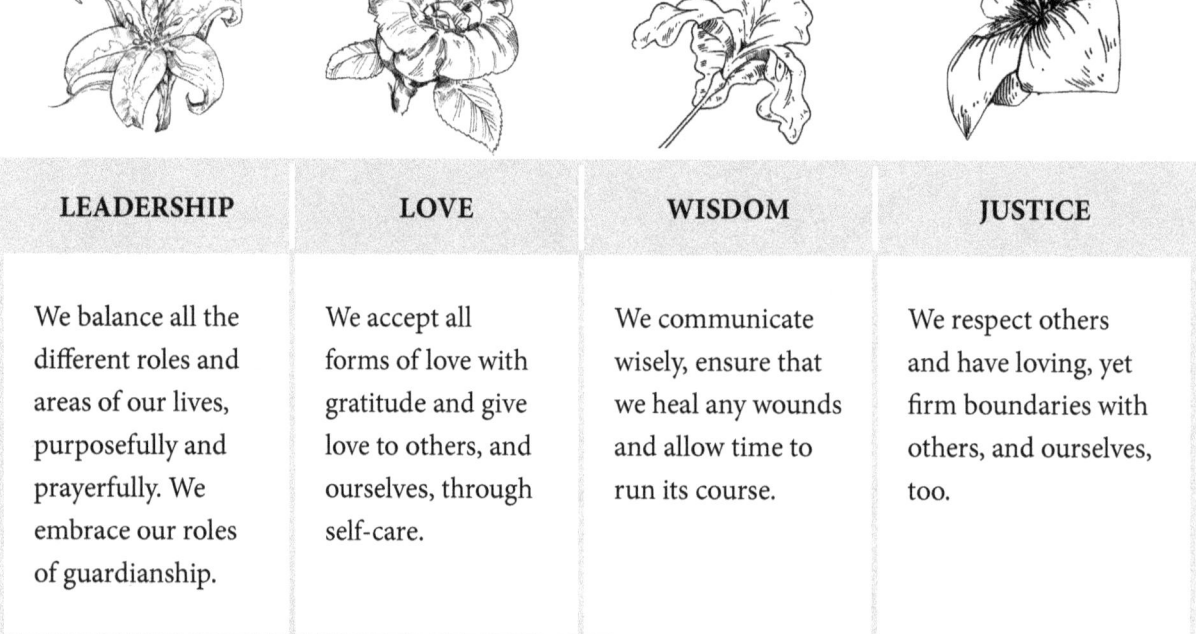

LEADERSHIP	LOVE	WISDOM	JUSTICE
We balance all the different roles and areas of our lives, purposefully and prayerfully. We embrace our roles of guardianship.	We accept all forms of love with gratitude and give love to others, and ourselves, through self-care.	We communicate wisely, ensure that we heal any wounds and allow time to run its course.	We respect others and have loving, yet firm boundaries with others, and ourselves, too.

Draw a line on each of the following vases to indicate how much of the four traits you have in your life. You may find some vases contain more than others, or perhaps some of them are overfilled; that's okay, as it provides you with an indication of where you need more balance.

Leadership   Love   Wisdom   Justice

Introduction

Foundations and Nourishment

The four traits of leadership, love, wisdom and justice manifest themselves in your life when you cultivate the following twelve habits. The first six make up the *foundations*, or bedrock, of your inner garden. This bedrock consists of the fundamental habits of all good spouses. The remaining six habits give *nourishment* to the soil of your garden: for your garden to flourish, you need nourished soil. These are The Twelve Habits of Highly Cherished Muslimahs!

FOUNDATION HABITS	NOURISHING HABITS
1. Purpose	7. Guardianship
2. Balance	8. Giving Love
3. Gratitude	9. Healing
4. Self-Care	10. Time
5. Communication	11. Self-Respect
6. Respecting Others	12. Self-Discipline

The Four Traits of a Cherished Muslimah Workbook

    The six foundation habits need to be established before everything else to support the topsoil and sustain growth. A solid foundation ensures that you are a purposeful, balanced woman, grateful and respectful of those around you, and an effective communicator! Once these foundations are established, we can then provide our gardens with nourishment by cultivating the remaining six habits, resulting in healthy and flourishing growth. Nourished soil ensures a life of love, growth and safety.

Twelve Healthy Habits to Cultivate

On the following pages, you will find descriptions of the six foundation habits and the six nourishing habits, as well as space for you to reflect on which ones you feel you need to establish or improve the most. Consider the following questions when completing the next exercise:

- Which habits do you struggle the most with?

- Why do you think you struggle with them?

- Which ones are you having the most success with?

- Why do you think you have success with them?

- When and how did you develop these successful habits?

- You may find that certain habits are non-existent, you may be practising no self-care at all, or you may have communication habits that aren't really working in your favour. If this is the case, how long have you struggled in these areas?

Foundation Habits

CONNECTING TO YOUR PURPOSE

We do everything purposefully in our lives, as an act of worshipping Allah and as an emulation of His Messenger ﷺ. We do our best, looking for ways to please Allah and to connect with His Messenger and leave the outcome with Him. We do everything prayerfully, knowing that only Allah gives success, and chooses the best for us.

A BALANCED LIFE

Our lives have many facets, and it is important to balance out each of them. Any area of our life that is given too much energy will become distorted, and it will have a negative impact on all other areas. Balance is the key.

GRATITUDE

We show gratitude for all the good we have in our lives and are open to receiving all the good that comes our way. We healthily express our desires so that our husbands know exactly how to love us.

SELF-CARE

When we look after ourselves first and foremost, we have enough energy and enthusiasm to fulfil all the responsibilities in our lives. We also look at overcoming obstacles to self-care.

COMMUNICATION

We communicate our desires, feelings, limitations and values effectively using 'I' messages. We build rapport with others and know how to phrase our requests for change. We know what to say and how to say it.

RESPECTING OTHERS

When we accept our husbands for who they are and understand why we all behave differently, we can then take control of our own lives instead of trying to control them. We also apologise to others when we don't treat them in the way they deserve to be treated.

Introduction

Exercise 0.4 Establishing Foundation Habits

CONNECTING TO YOUR PURPOSE

A BALANCED LIFE

GRATITUDE

SELF-CARE

COMMUNICATION

RESPECTING OTHERS

Nourishing Habits

GUARDIANSHIP

Embracing the different God-given roles that both husbands and wives have within the marriage, we work to create our own unique working balance, as every union is unique.

GIVING LOVE

We give love to our husbands using their preferred love language. Giving love also involves being generous with our admiration and tapping into our seductive feminine energy.

HEALING

We clear our inner gardens by healing our wounds and understanding the wounds of our husbands. We look at balancing the negative polarities of the four traits so that we can grow in a way that is good for both our husbands and us.

TIME

Our inner wisdom shows us exactly when the right time is to do and say things, and when we should let things lie. We learn from the past and utilise the experiences we have had to our benefit. We learn to understand the changing seasons of life.

SELF-RESPECT

Respect works both ways: once you know how to respect others, you can uphold that respect for yourself. Your inner garden needs fences to keep the bad stuff out. Having self-respect means you look to fulfil your own needs if they are not being met.

SELF-DISCIPLINE

We have boundaries with ourselves, knowing that by either doing too much or doing too little, we can harm ourselves and our families. With self-discipline, a woman can support her husband by creating a home using her own strengths and talents.

Introduction

Exercise 0.5 Establishing Nourishing Habits

GUARDIANSHIP

GIVING LOVE

HEALING

TIME

SELF-RESPECT

SELF-DISCIPLINE

Exercise 0.6 What's Working and What's Not

Reflect on what is working in your life and what is not working. Ask yourself what you want instead. Defining what you want is the first step towards getting to where you want. It provides direction, a destination. *Remember to speak for yourself* and what YOU want, and *not what you want from your husband.* Also, make sure you have *realistic expectations*—so instead of writing 'I don't want to ever argue again', perhaps write, 'I want to handle conflict in a constructive way'.

WHAT'S WORKING

WHAT'S NOT WORKING

WHAT I WANT INSTEAD

Introduction

Exercise 0.7 How Does Your Garden Grow?

Be soft like soil and grow colourful flowers.

Mawlana Rumi

Which flowers grow in your garden? Does the lily grow, the fertile queen, prominently and fragrantly growing regardless of those around her? What about the rose: does she bloom in your garden, using her thorns to protect herself as well as hooking on to all those around her with her charm and fragrance? Does the iris have a place in your garden, with her wisdom and colourful rainbows? And surely your garden cannot be complete without the long, protective swords of the gladiolus, symbolising security and self-restraint? Reflect below on which flowers are blooming in your garden, which need extra nourishment and which ones need to be planted. It's time to tend to your garden.

LILY

Symbolises life and fertility, prominence and royalty; blooms if that is what is decreed for her. She flourishes when supported by the masculine…

ROSE

Symbolises love and openness, self-protection and the ability to 'capture' with her love hooks. Flourishing from small buds of gratitude, she trails beauty and perfume all around her…

IRIS

Symbolising wisdom, she has the ability to seek out the healing and benefit in every hardship. Her flexibility gives her the ability to adjust to her environment…

GLADIOLUS

Symbolises protection and safety. Her sword-like leaves protect her from harm, and her sheath ensures that she only uses her strength for good…

The Lord of the Cherished Muslimah

Allah has ninety-nine names, one-hundred less one; and he who believes in their meanings and acts accordingly will enter Paradise.

Bukhari (7392)

Allah has 99 names. Well, He has many more, some which we know of and some which we are unaware of, but in the above narration, we are told about 99 specific names. I feel blessed to have been given the ability by Allah to have memorised His names by heart and to have recited them to my teacher, Shaykh Sulayman Van Ael, who learnt them from his teacher, with this process going back all the way to the Messenger of Allah ﷺ. Through coaching, I help women connect with Allah's names, as by doing this we can ensure that we are always connected to not only our purpose, but Allah's power as well.

We can connect with Allah through His names by:

1. Putting certain names into practice in our lives; such as Ash-Shakūr, by being generous to others, and Al-Wadūd, by loving others as unconditionally as we can.
2. Putting the *opposite* into practice and *submitting* to the names that we can't put into practice; such as Al-Mutakabbir, by submitting to Allah being higher than everything else, and Al-Jabbar, by submitting to Him when He breaks us in order to make us.

Through which of His names can you connect with Him, in order to manifest the four traits in your life? His names of majesty, power and greatness can help us connect to our leadership trait, by acknowledging that we are leaders in our own domains yet never above Allah's sovereignty. His names of love and generosity can help us practise being loving and giving to others (and ourselves). The names of Allah's knowledge, wisdom and support can help us connect with our inner wisdom, and His names of accountability, reprimand and power can help us connect with our justice trait.

Reading and learning about Allah's names and attributes is one of the ways you can get to know Him, for how can we worship Him if we don't know Him? Connecting to Allah through His names, via books and teachers, will connect us to Him and give us the keys with which to invoke Him with, as each of His names is a key to a door. He has commanded us to invoke Him by His names, so let's do it!

And to Allah belong the most beautiful names, so invoke Him by them!

Al-A'raf (7:180)

Introduction

The Messenger of Allah ﷺ said *'man ahsāhā dakhal al jannah'* meaning whoever does *ahsāh* of these names will enter Jannah. This word has loosely been translated as 'to have memorised'. Alhamdulillah! A ticket to paradise, for memorising the names of Allah—what more could one ask for? Yet, our teachers tell us that it is not enough to have just memorised them. *Ahsāh* means to:

1. Understand them
2. Memorise them
3. Put them into practice in our daily lives
4. Invoke Allah by and supplicate to Him with them

And this is where the challenge lies. How often are we guilty of forgetting Allah's names and attributes, resulting in us inadvertently suffering? Do we even know what His attributes are? Without knowing them, our connection to Him will be weaker. Yet every single name of Allah, when said with the presence of the heart and mind, has an immediate transformational effect on us. Each name empowers us, as we see Allah's hand in shaping us, in making us, in His giving, and in His taking away. We see Allah looking after us, guiding us, protecting us and nourishing us.

And so, although I'm not a scholar or an expert in this field, at the beginning of each chapter, I have attempted to identify which of Allah's names we can connect with when cultivating the twelve habits in our lives, and for each habit you will find a small compilation of Allah's names to connect to (twelve each, to be precise!) by putting them into practice or submitting to them, and also supplicating to Allah with them. The compilations are just my attempts to group the names in an empowering and healing way—you may feel that some additional names of Allah should be included in the lists, and if so, please add them yourself. Better still, write them in underneath! A full list of the 99 names is included in the Appendix.

Foundations

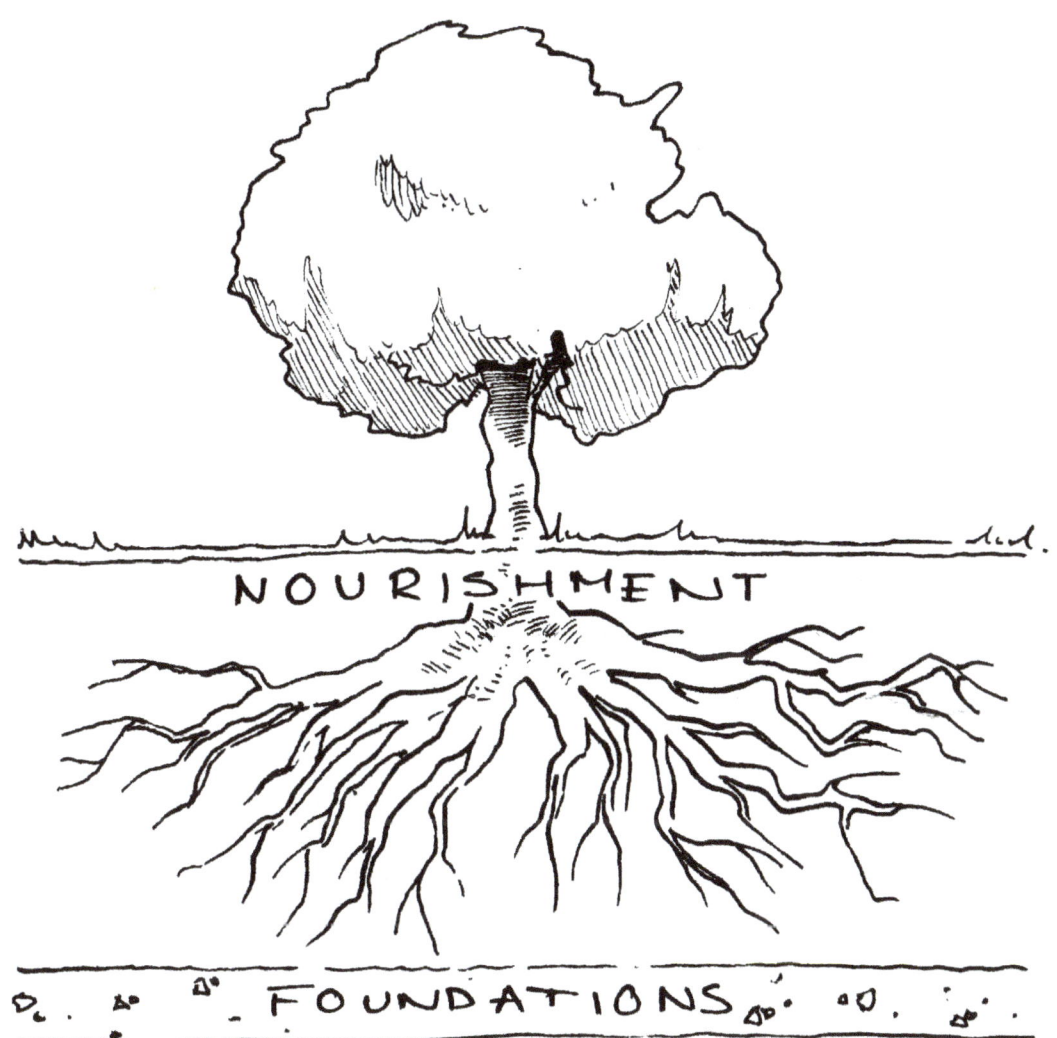

Foundations

When the foundations of marriage are not established, life is an exhausting experience. With a lack of leadership skills, you may end up doing more than your fair share of work in the family, to the point of burn-out. Those around you may be complacent and any work that you delegate may be inadequately done, making you feel that it would be easier if you just did everything yourself! It is hard to show gratitude for the gifts in your life, as you may not get many. With poor communication skills, your limits are seldom respected, as you never manage to convey them effectively, and everything you say is misunderstood. Lacking self-love and awareness, you can't remember the last time you had time to yourself. Even if you did have some time alone, you wouldn't know what to do with it! Weak foundations mean that both you and your husband would rather do your own things than spend time with one another. They paint a very bleak picture...!

Yet, when you have an established foundation in your marriage, life becomes rich and fulfilling. As you bring leadership, love, wisdom and justice to your marriage, respect is cultivated between you and your husband. You take time out to relax and those around you take pleasure in helping you lighten your workload, which gives you more time to do the things you love to do. You become a woman who knows what she wants and can communicate effectively. A strong foundation provides the base to let the masterpiece of your life flourish, and this section looks at how to establish this through the four traits.

In this section of the workbook, we will look at how to establish the following six habits in your life, starting with Connecting to Your Purpose.

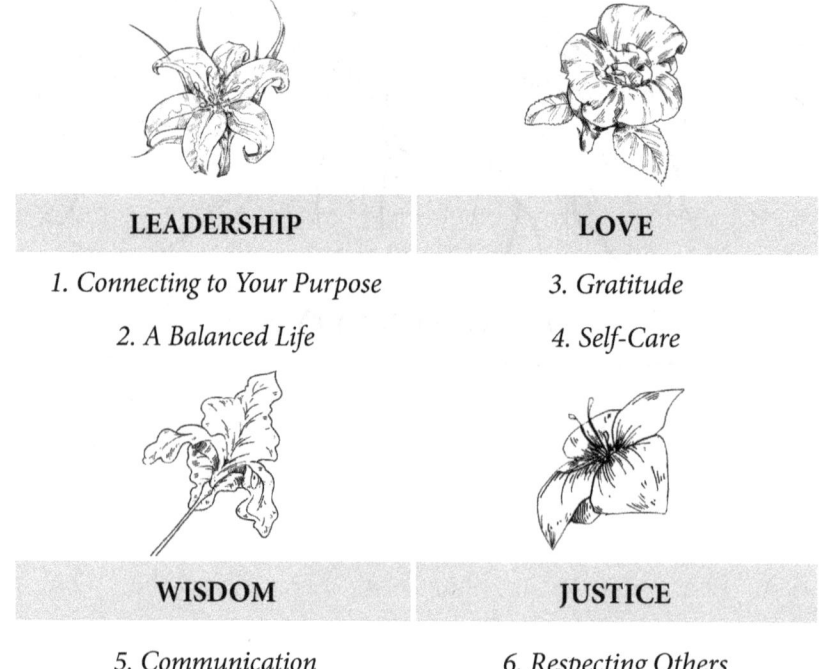

LEADERSHIP	**LOVE**
1. Connecting to Your Purpose	*3. Gratitude*
2. A Balanced Life	*4. Self-Care*

WISDOM	**JUSTICE**
5. Communication	*6. Respecting Others*

LEADERSHIP

1. Connecting to Your Purpose

2. A Balanced Life

Leadership

1. Connecting to Your Purpose

*Be like the lily in your purpose: stand out,
do your best and bloom when Allah wants you to.*

*Recommended Reading Point: The Four Traits of a Cherished Muslimah:
Introduction to Leadership (page 19) & Chapter 1 - Connecting to Your Purpose*

This habit connects everything you do to servitude, by learning to intend any act as an expression of your slavehood to Allah. It shows you how to uncover the values beneath your goals and create powerful intentions with those values. You will create two plans: how you want to be cherished by Allah and which ways you want to emulate and express your love for Allah's Messenger ﷺ. And then, with your intentions and plans in place, you will take them to Allah and articulate them into heartfelt prayers.

For the like of this, let the workers work.

As-Saffaat (37:61)

What is your purpose for wanting to improve your marriage? What do you intend to do with these new habits? While improving your relationship with your husband and cultivating a deep love and closeness between the two of you are beautiful, desired outcomes, they will only bring true satisfaction when they are done as a form of *worship* and *love* and as a form of *emulation* of the Messenger of Allah ﷺ.

For those who do good is the best reward and more!

Yunus (10:26)

By continuing to connect to your purpose and doing everything worshipfully, you will be happy to sacrifice more than you may previously have been prepared to. You will be able to let go of perfection, knowing that it is your intention that counts. Living purposefully will ensure that you do everything for Allah's pleasure. Anything you sacrifice is for Him, and the reward for that *is* Him. Not only will the ones who do good get the best reward (Paradise) but they will get *more*... beholding Allah, looking at His noble face. He is Ash-Shakūr, the One who gives in abundance, even more than we deserve. And so you won't mind being the first one to change.

By knowing the Messenger of Allah ﷺ, emulating him and sending blessings on him, you will ensure your constant connection with him, receive his prayers and intercession, be guaranteed to be cherished by Allah and forgiven your sins. And that is how to be a Cherished Muslimah!

Say: If you love Allah, then follow me, Allah will love you and forgive you your sins, and Allah is forgiving and merciful.

Al-Baqarah (3:31)

The Divine Names for Purposeful Living

When you create a purposeful life by connecting to Allah through His names, you acknowledge that He is your purpose for everything, as He created you, is the highest, the first and the last. He possesses all majesty and power and never perishes. He is the one purpose and intention. When establishing your purpose habit, connect to Allah through His names of majesty and sovereignty by putting them into practice/submitting to them, and call upon Him with them when you pray to Him.

	PURPOSE
ALLAH (1)	The one who unites all the attributes of divinity
AL-MALIK (4)	The king, ruler
AL-MUTAKABBIR (11)	He who is elevated above all
AL-KHĀLIQ (12)	The creator
AL-ALĪ (37)	The high, above Him there is no rank or status
AL-KABĪR (38)	The great, in essence and existence, without comparison
AL-MĀJID (66)	Name of majesty, all glorious, noble, beautiful, bountiful, more emphatic
AL-WĀHID (67)	He who is alone, no one shares in His oneness
AL-AHAD (68)	The one
AL-MUTA'ĀLI (78)	He who is elevated above all, intensified of Al-Alī
AL-MĀLIK AL-MULK (84)	The possessor of all the world
DHUL JALĀL WAL-IKRĀM (85)	The possessor of majesty and generosity
AR-RASHĪD (98)	He who does the best

How do you define worship?

Whatever you sow, sow for God, who has no end,
Because you are captive of that beloved friend.

Mawlana Rumi

The word 'worship' has many meanings and connotations and the way we worship Allah is often dependent on what we think the word means. For me, it was a verb, and 'to worship' meant to pray to the one who had created me, and in worshipping Him, He would look after me. Yet decades later, I learnt that He was looking after me whether I worshipped Him or not—He was *that* giving and merciful. The Arabic word for 'worship' is *ibadah* which comes from the word *abd*, meaning slave. When the word 'worship' is seen in this light, it becomes an act of slavehood and servitude towards one's master.

Think of the way a human slave is with his human master. He wants to please him and keep him happy, out of fear of being punished and hope for being taken care of. If that is the way a slave is with a human master, what about when you acknowledge Allah as your Master: the loving, merciful, giving, generous Master? How much more would the slave want to please the true Master, who provides for the slave and gives him more than he deserves, for no other reason except that the slave was grateful? Who overlooks and pardons, and if He punishes, He punishes less than the slave truly deserves?

When you connect your actions with a worshipful attitude, you can do things simply because you are Allah's slave and He is your Master. You do what He says and follow His commands. This attitude turns every action into a form of slavehood, a demonstration of how you are a slave to Allah, and only care to worship Him.

Do you remember Mariya from page 27 of *The Four Traits of a Cherished Muslimah*? When she was tired, she put her feet up and relaxed, knowing she could continue to serve Allah after she was rested. Yet when we connect with our purpose, we make the intention to please Allah while we are resting, moving continuously from one act of worship to the next.

So when you are finished, strive on. And to your Lord turn your attention.

Al Inshirah (94:7–8)

Leadership

Exercise 1.1 Defining Worship

What does 'worship' mean to you?

Exercise 1.2 *Purposeful Intentions*

The (reward of) deeds, depend upon the intentions and every person will get the reward according to what he has intended.

Bukhari (1)

Reflect on what your intentions are for improving your marriage. A good question to ponder on is: what do I want and what is important about getting it? After this, connect your values to Allah. Remember, by connecting them to worship, love and emulation, you will always be spiritually satisfied, enabling you to remain centred on what is really important.

WHAT DO I WANT?	WHAT IS IMPORTANT ABOUT GETTING IT?	MY INTENTION WITH ALLAH
e.g. To be loved in my marriage.	*To enjoy the gift of love and tranquillity that Allah has put between two spouses.*	*To create a marriage where there is love and tranquillity.*

Why Me?

Oh changer of the hearts, make my heart firm upon Your religion. Verily, there is no human being except that his heart is between two fingers of the fingers of Allah, so whomsoever He wills He makes steadfast, and whomever He wills He causes to deviate.

Tirmidhi (3522)

Some of the first questions I get asked by ladies embarking on a journey to improve their marriage are: 'Why me?', 'Why do I have to do all of this?' and 'Surely if I'm the one doing all of the changing, I'm telling him that I'm the one with the problem and not him?' My response to this is the NLP presupposition which states that when one person changes, the other person cannot not change. When we choose to be the better person, we inspire others to want to be better. The opposite is also true. When we behave from our lowest, egotistic selves, our bad energy encourages us to contract and retaliate. Ask yourself: when presented with a test and trial, which path will you take? The path to stagnation, where the land is barren, or the path to change, cultivation and growth?

It's your choice when you come to that crossroad: which path will you choose?

And if you want to take steps towards positive change (and it is obvious that you do, or you wouldn't be reading this book!), it is only because Allah has inspired you to do that. Your heart is in Allah's hands, and if He wishes, He can make you steadfast or deviate; therefore, if you find yourself guided to change your condition, know that this is your good fortune and provision from Allah. Instead of thinking 'Why me?', a Cherished Muslimah says, 'Ya Rabbi, thank you for choosing me!'

Exercise 1.3 Why Me?

He gives wisdom to whom He wills, and whoever has been given wisdom has certainly been given much good.

Al-Baqarah (2:269)

Guidance is a bestowal from Allah. It is a gift, not an entitlement. Reflect on how it is in your best interest to take the first steps to lead. Reflect on how the Messenger of Allah ﷺ took the initiative to do things, guided others and inspired them to change.

Live Prayerfully

> *There is no Muslim who supplicates to Allah [...]*
> *but that Allah will give him one of three answers:*
> *He will hasten the fulfilment of his supplication, He will store it for him in the hereafter,*
> *or He will divert an evil from him similar to it.*
>
> *Musnad Ahmad (10749)*

Once you know what you want and why you want it, pray for it! Prayer is an amazing gift from Allah. Not only is He the answerer of prayers, but He also promises us that He will always answer our prayers in the best of ways for us: by fulfilling our supplication, giving it to us in the Hereafter, or diverting an evil from us. It is this conviction that will bring us true satisfaction from our prayers to Him.

Send abundant salawat (blessings) upon the Messenger of Allah ﷺ, asking Allah to bless him and grant him peace, as we were told by the Messenger of Allah ﷺ that constant salawat upon him would take care of all our worries.

> *Ubayy asked: 'Should I make all of my prayers for you?'*
> *He replied: 'If you do that, then your problems would be solved*
> *and your sins would be forgiven.'*
>
> *Tirmidhi (2457)*

Once you have made your prayer, have absolute certainty that it has been answered in the way Allah has decreed. How many lives have been transformed by prayer? How many times has Allah answered our calls in ways better than we could have hoped for? For me, this is the real and only law of attraction. If you want something, pray for it; if you don't know what you want, still pray! Ask Allah for help and clarity and let Him sort it all out for you.

> *Call on Allah while having absolute certainty that He will answer.*
>
> *Tirmidhi (3479)*

Exercise 1.4 Prayerful Intentions

Whenever He releases your tongue to ask, know that He wants to give to you.

Hikam – Ibn Ata illah (102)

Reflect on your intentions with Allah and what you need to do to achieve these. What changes will you need to make in your life? After this, pray to Allah for it. Ask Him and beg Him to give you the ability to make these changes. Ask Him to help you and facilitate your affairs for you, and to make it easy to achieve your goal. Ask Him for whatever you feel will help you!

MY INTENTION	STEPS TO TAKE TO ACHIEVE MY INTENTION	MY PRAYER
e.g. To create a marriage where there is love and tranquility	1. Communicate effectively 2. Don't sweat the small stuff 3. Don't remain stagnant/always better yourself	Oh Allah, help me to communicate effectively, to remember what is important and to continuously better myself

The Four Traits of a Cherished Muslimah Workbook

How to Be a Cherished Muslimah

I know I make it sound easy
But He's always there believe me
When you keep going the extra mile
Expect God to make it worth your while.

———

Zain Bhikha

I love this term—being a Cherished Muslimah. In my opinion, women have been given too many titles: A Righteous Wife, An Obedient Wife, A Surrendered Wife, A Fascinating Woman, etc. Each title conjures up a stereotype which many of us are unwilling to accept: 'I don't want to be a doormat', 'I don't want to live my life in submission to my husband', 'I'm more than just a wife/mother' or 'I want to be my own version of a woman'. I've often said these same commonly-heard phrases myself!

Yet here I am, proposing another title! A Cherished Muslimah! Cherished by whom, though? Often we make the mistake of assuming that if we are the best versions of ourselves, then other people will, in return, be the best versions of themselves with us too. Sadly, it doesn't always work like that.

Every single encounter we have with others is a transaction.1 You give something to someone, even if it is as simple as a greeting, and you get something back. In a marriage, a man and woman come together to live happily with love, doing things intentionally to please one another. You give love, and you get love back, and your love increases for one another until you walk off holding hands into the sunset, InshaAllah.

Yet it doesn't always work that way. Sometimes all you get back is a feeling of hurt. So what do you do when your love, efforts and respect are not reciprocated? Do you stop when you don't get anything in return? It is important to realign yourself with your purpose and intention: you are loving, putting in the effort and respecting others in order to be loved by Allah. He sees you. Everything you do. Every endeavour and every gesture of love and respect. And as you continue to draw closer to Him with your extra (supererogatory) efforts, He loves you.

My servant continues to draw near to Me with supererogatory works so that I shall love him.

———

Bukhari (6502)

Exercise 1.5 How to Be a Cherished Muslimah

In terms of the four traits, reflect on all you can do to gain Allah's love, so you are a woman who submits herself to her Lord, and is loved by Him: A Cherished Muslimah. What can you do, how can you be? How can you nourish your marriage in ways that please Him? The paths to Allah are many. Which paths do you choose to take to gain His pleasure and love? Through which of His names can you connect to Him, be it through invocation, reflection or submission?

LEADERSHIP	*e.g. Getting everyone to help out while preparing a meal – staying calm, delegating tasks, and leading by example by being a part of it.*
LOVE	*e.g. Giving your child a hug and kiss every morning to show her that she is loved and cherished. You please Allah for showing love and mercy to the child He has given you.*
WISDOM	*e.g. Holding back in moments of anger to remain silent and later to respond with kindness and forgiveness to embody the character of the Messenger of Allah ﷺ.*
JUSTICE	*e.g. Standing up for yourself when someone says something painful to you. You please Allah by protecting yourself from being hurt.*

The Four Traits of a Cherished Muslimah Workbook

Exercise 1.6 Your Personal Love Plan

No, by Him in Whose Hand my soul is, (you will not have complete faith) till I am dearer to you than your own self.

Bukhari (6632)

The companions of the Messenger of Allah ﷺ had unique ways of expressing their love for him: through serving him, giving charity, helping the needy, making him laugh, sending gifts to him, loving his family, or simply loving things he loved! In which ways will you follow the Messenger of Allah ﷺ? Will you emulate the things he did? Will you follow his teachings? Will you keep your connection to him by sending blessings upon him, as he advised us to, and as Allah ordered us to? The paths to love are also many, and the result is being cherished by Allah, the Lord of the Worlds!

Love Allah for what He nourishes you with of His blessings, love me for the love of Allah and love the people of my house for my love.

Tirmidhi (3789)

Take this opportunity to make your own personalised plan of how you will love him ﷺ so that he becomes dearer to you than your own self.

Leadership

Exercise 1.7 A Prayerful Purpose

In this section, you have started to establish a purposeful habit by looking at how to do things worshipfully and prayerfully. You have looked at the different ways that you can please Allah so that He loves you, and reflected on how you can love His Messenger ﷺ in your own way. Revisit all of your intentions and goals for this habit and turn them into prayers. Invoke Allah by His names of majesty and rulership. Use these prayers to ask Allah daily with full conviction that every prayer is answered. You will be doing this for all twelve habits, InshaAllah.

GOALS & INTENTIONS	MY PRAYERS
DEFINING WORSHIP	
WORSHIPFUL INTENTIONS	
LIVING PRAYERFULLY	
BEING A CHERISHED MUSLIMAH	
MY PERSONAL LOVE PLAN	

2. A Balanced Life

*Be like the lily in balance: be in effortless harmony
with other flowers, despite being the queen.*

*Recommended Reading Point: The Four Traits of a Cherished Muslimah:
Chapter 2 - A Balanced Life*

In this chapter, we focus on balancing the four traits and also the different *areas* of our lives by understanding that whenever we are excessive in any particular trait or area, the neglected one will become deficient and suffer. This chapter looks at bringing balance to the neglected traits and areas. Like a gardener who walks around her garden and inspects which areas are neglected, you can identify these traits and areas and then take the steps needed to cultivate and nourish them. In this chapter, you will also reflect on how the Messenger of Allah ﷺ was the perfect balance of the four traits and how he ﷺ manifested them in his life.

The Divine Names for a Balanced Life

When you balance your life by connecting to Allah through His names, you acknowledge that He proportions everything in a perfect balance. He is the one who is merciful to all—not just a certain group. In doing this, you ensure you balance the different roles in your life, including the role of giving rights to your own body. You submit to His perfect balance and His ability to bring everything together in harmony, and in doing so, strive to bring balance and harmony into your life. When establishing your balance habit, connect to Allah through His names of balance, perfection and equity, by putting them into practice/submitting to them, and call upon Him with them when you pray to Him.

BALANCE	
ALLAH (1)	The one who unites all the attributes of divinity
AL-QUDŪS (5)	The flawless, transcends every attribute of perfection
AS-SALĀM (6)	He who is perfect, flawless, free from any insufficiency
AL-QĀBID (21)	He who takes away
AL-BĀSIT (22)	He who spreads out
AL-KHĀFID (23)	He who brings down
AR-RĀFI (24)	He who raises up
AL-ADL (30)	He who is just in rulings and proportions
AL-MUBDI (59)	The one who starts things
AL-MUĪ'D (60)	The one who brings things back
AL-MUQADDIM (71)	He who makes things happen, promotes them
AL-MU'AKHIR (72)	He who delays things, pushes them away
AS-SABŪR (99)	He who does everything at the right time

Exercise 2.1 Balance Your Traits

With each of the traits, we can be balanced, in excess or in deficiency. They're a bit like our vitamin levels—too much or too little can actually harm us and stop us from living healthily. When we are not balanced, we fluctuate between being overactive and passive in the traits. For example, if a leader is not balanced, she will fluctuate between being a tyrant and a weak leader, going from one extreme to the other until she makes a conscious effort to balance out her life. Like a pendulum that swings from one side to the other, we keep fluctuating until we finally recentre and be still; embracing balance, wholeness, fullness.

Flipping between the two polarities

Once you start being excessive or deficient in any of the traits, you find yourself 'flipping' from one extreme to the other. Pay particular attention when you start flipping between the two polarities and focus on becoming balanced.

As I wrote on page 35 of *The Four Traits of a Cherished Muslimah,* I have a tendency to alternate from giving too much love and not giving any, and I normally start off the whole process by being excessive in the love trait. Pay attention to which extreme polarity you start off with when you start to 'flip' between the two extremes—this is probably the one you need to balance.

In Chapter 2 of *The Four Traits of a Cherished Muslimah,* we read about the healthy characteristics of each trait, and what happens when we are either excessive or deficient in them. Record on the next page how balanced you are in the four traits. As each trait has three habits to cultivate, mark each habit out on each trait's balance scale which will give you an idea of how balanced you are in that trait.

If you have a tendency to be more excessive in certain habits, mark that habit towards the left-hand side of the balance scale, with +10 being the most excessive. If you are quite balanced, then mark the habit towards the middle, where the flower is—that's where and when you will enjoy the fruits and beauty of that habit: when you are balanced. If you are deficient in a habit, then mark it towards the right-hand side of the balance scale, with -10 being the most deficient.

You can bring yourself back to balance by reading the specific parts of *The Four Traits of a Cherished Muslimah* and cultivating the traits in which you are excessive or deficient. Here's an example of my leadership balance scale—as you can see, I have a tendency to become excessive in my balance (B) and guardianship (Gu) habits, but MashaAllah I'm doing alright with my purpose (P):

+10 +5 *Leadership* -5 -10
       GU B   P

THE 3 HABITS OF LEADERSHIP		
Purpose (P)	Balance (B)	Guardianship (Gu)

Four Traits - Balance Scales

Balancing excesses and deficiencies in Leadership

`+10   +5   Leadership   -5   -10`

Place (P) (B) (Gu) on the scale above

EXCESSIVENESS	THE 3 HABITS OF LEADERSHIP	DEFICIENCY
All actions and striving are to attain an outcome	(P) Actions connect to purpose	Unable to strive as the goal seems unattainable
Hyper-focusing on certain areas and ignoring the rest	(B) Balanced life in all areas	Neglecting responsibilities due to overwhelm
Obsessing and controlling over one's charges	(Gu) Embrace roles of guardianship	Neglect and lack of control of one's charges

Balancing excesses and deficiencies in Love

`+10   +5   Love   -5   -10`

Place (Gr) (SC) (GL) on the scale above

EXCESSIVENESS	THE 3 HABITS OF LOVE	DEFICIENCY
Unappreciative of many blessings one has	(Gr) Show gratitude for what you have	Feeling unworthy of any blessings
Too much self-care	(SC) Exercise healthy self-care	Not enough self-care
Giving too much love	(GL) Give healthy love	Not having any love to give

Balancing excesses and deficiencies in Wisdom

+10   +5   Wisdom   -5   -10

Place (C) (H) (T) on the scale above

EXCESSIVENESS	THE 3 HABITS OF WISDOM	DEFICIENCY
Communicate for personal benefit	(C) Communicate wisely	Unable to communicate to one's detriment
Stubborn refusal to heal	(H) Heal your wounds	Perceived inability to heal
Wanting results immediately	(T) Allow time to run its course	Unable to make changes to the current situation

Balancing excesses and deficiencies in Justice

+10   +5   Justice   -5   -10

Place (RO) (SR) (SD) on the scale above

EXCESSIVENESS	THE 3 HABITS OF JUSTICE	DEFICIENCY
Controlling others' lives	(RO) Respect others	Being controlled by others
Putting own needs and wants above everyone else's	(SR) Respect yourself	Prioritising the needs of others to one's own detriment
Doing too much	(SD) Exercise self-discipline	Doing too little

Leadership

Exercise 2.2 How Full are Your Love Tanks?

The secret to staying in touch with our true selves is to keep filling up our love tanks.

John Gray

In order to have a nourished and healthy life, there are certain areas in which you need to be fulfilled. Similar to the four traits, if you are excessive or deficient in any of them (just like vitamins) then your life and well-being will suffer. Interestingly, the other areas of your life will suffer too. In his book, *How To Get What You Want And Want What You Have,* John Gray calls these areas 'love tanks' and explains that it is essential to keep filling them up in order to be whole and complete. These are the areas we need love from and need to give love to.

Fill in the following table, and reflect upon how full or fulfilled your love tanks are, aiming to fill each one up to 100%. You may notice that you dedicate more time and energy to certain areas of your life while other areas are being neglected. Each time you fill one tank, focus on filling one that isn't as full. If you feel dissatisfied in an area that is already full, it is probably due to the emptiness you feel in the neglected areas of your life, so work on filling them up, as mentioned in the Connecting to Your Purpose chapter, moving from one act of worship to the next.

LOVE TANKS	% FULL/ FULFILLED	HOW TO FILL (IF DEPLETED)
ALLAH		
FAMILY		
FRIENDS		
SELF		
MARRIAGE		
DEPENDANTS		
COMMUNITY/ CAREER		

Exercise 2.3 The Perfect Balance ﷺ

Recommended Reading Point: The Four Traits of a Cherished Muslimah: Preface & A Balanced Life - Chapter 2

The above triangles show the composition of the four traits for the male, or masculine energy. These are slightly different from the structure of women's traits, with the main difference being that a man has a stronger association to justice than love, whereas a woman has a natural affinity to love than justice.[2]

Yet the concept is the same: balancing the four traits leads to a whole, perfect person; balancing these four traits is the winning formula!

It is often hard (if not impossible) to find someone who can be classed as the perfect example. Mankind searches for perfect role models to find inspiration and yet, time and time again, we are sorely disappointed when the ones we look up to let us down. Fortunately, as Muslims, we have the perfect person to raise onto the pedestal, someone who will never let us down or disappoint us: the Messenger of Allah ﷺ.

Verily in the Messenger of Allah you have an excellent example for everyone whose hope is in Allah and the last day, and remembers Allah abundantly.

Al-Ahzab (33:21)

Reading the biography of the Messenger of Allah ﷺ and learning about his character is an excellent starting point to fall in love with the best of creation. Learning about him ﷺ through books and teachers shows us how he embodied all four traits of leadership, love, wisdom and justice.

The Perfect Balance

Take this opportunity to write down what you know about the Messenger of Allah ﷺ: his leadership qualities, his justice, his wisdom and his love. Reflect on how he was indeed the perfect embodiment of the four traits. If you don't know about his ﷺ characteristics, use this opportunity to find out more about him, as only through knowing him can we emulate him.

LEADERSHIP	LOVE	WISDOM	JUSTICE

Exercise 2.4 A Prayerful Balance

To develop a habit of balance, you have looked at the ways that you can balance the four traits in your life, and how the Messenger of Allah ﷺ had the perfect balance of all four. Similar to what you did for the previous habit, it's time to pray for it! Invoke Allah by His names for His guidance. Revisit all of your intentions and goals for this habit and turn them into prayers:

GOALS & INTENTIONS	MY PRAYERS
BALANCING MY TRAITS	
FILLING MY LOVE TANKS	
THE PERFECT BALANCE ﷺ	

LOVE

3. Gratitude

4. Self-Care

Love

3. Gratitude

Be like the rose in gratitude:
allow your small buds to flourish with gratitude for every blessing.

Recommended Reading Point: The Four Traits of a Cherished Muslimah:
Introduction to Love (page 77) & Chapter 4 – Gratitude

We often miss out on opportunities to connect with one another due to missing the blessings that are under our very noses! This part of the workbook shows us how to cultivate the habit of gratitude and helps us to identify what types of things to look out for.

The Divine Names for Gratitude

When you cultivate the habit of gratitude by connecting to Allah through His names, you acknowledge that it is He who has designed everything so perfectly for you. He is the generous, the bestower of provision and gifts. He is the one who nourishes you with all the blessings you have in your life. You realise that gratitude brings life back into relationships with others and you are ever grateful to Him. When your loved ones praise you, you thank them and direct the praise back to Him. You show gratitude and connect to Allah by continually forgiving those around you and being enriched through Him. When establishing your gratitude habit, connect to Allah through His names of generosity, benefaction and bounty, by putting them into practice/submitting to them, and call upon Him with them when you pray to Him.

GRATITUDE	
ALLAH (1)	The one who unites all the attributes of divinity
AL-MUHAYMIN (8)	He who encompasses needs/wants
AL-WAHĀB (17)	The bestower of gifts
AR-RAZZĀQ (18)	The giver, provider
AL-ADL (30)	He who is just in rulings and proportions
ASH-SHAKŪR (36)	He who gives more than one deserves
AL-MUQĪT (40)	The maintainer and nourisher of food and knowledge
AL-KARĪM (43)	He who gives before you ask
AL-WADŪD (48)	He who loves unconditionally
AL-HAMĪD (57)	He who praises Himself
DHUL JALĀL WAL-IKRĀM (85)	The possessor of majesty and generosity
AL-GHANĪ (88)	The rich, independent
AL-MUGHNĪ (89)	He who enriches you

Gratitude for Being Me

Our Lord! Grant us good in this world and good in the hereafter.

Al-Baqarah (2:201)

Before showing gratitude to our husbands for all the good that they do, it is important for us to show gratitude to Allah for all the good He has given us as individuals, and to accept our gifts and talents!

On the following page, take a moment to reflect on your skills, qualities, talents and physical features, which are a blessing and an asset to your being. Please note that this is not being boastful or vain; rather, it is acknowledging the special bounties you have been blessed with. It is time to take stock of the richness of being you by expressing your gratitude to Allah!

And my success is not but through Allah. Upon Him I have relied, and to Him I return.

Hud (11:88)

This is an exercise in vulnerability—it is about taking ownership of the good that you have been blessed with. Once we accept what is good about us, when others mention it, we don't discount them or make excuses! Instead, we smile, and thank them for seeing the good in us, and we praise and thank Allah for His blessings and beg Him to increase us in all that is good.

Do not put in minimisers such as 'I'm okay at' or 'I could be better at'. Use words such as 'Allah has blessed me with an amazing ability to cook', 'Allah has given me the ability to sew', 'Allah has blessed me with beautiful hair' or 'Allah has blessed me with a melodious voice'. Take a moment of gratitude for being you!

This is by the grace of my Lord!
To test me whether I am grateful or ungrateful!

Al-Naml (27:40)

The Four Traits of a Cherished Muslimah Workbook

Exercise 3.1 Gratitude for Being Me

Give from your Master back to your Master.

Turkish Proverb

Make a list below of all your skills, qualities, talents and physical features which are a blessing and an asset to your being, and then thank Allah for blessing you with them! Take this opportunity to make the intention to only use your blessings to please Allah, never in a way that would displease Him. Allah encourages us to use our blessings in His cause by asking, *'Who is he that will loan to Allah a beautiful loan?'* (2:245). Therefore, utilise every blessing you have in His cause. If He blessed you with a beautiful voice, sing His praises! If He gave you the gift of mercy and compassion, visit those who need comfort. If He gave you wealth, use it to help those who have less than you. Give from the blessings that you receive from Him back to His world.

	MY BLESSINGS AND ASSETS, SKILLS, QUALITIES, TALENTS AND PHYSICAL FEATURES	HOW I CAN PLEASE ALLAH WITH THEM
	e.g. I have beautiful eyes, Alhamdulillah.	*By only looking at what is good, and striving to see the good in others.*
1		
2		
3		
4		
5		
6		
7		
8		
9		
10		

Love

Exercise 3.2 Things I Am Grateful for in My Husband

Then which of the favours of your Lord will you deny?

Ar-Rahman (55:13)

Many ladies who want to fix their marriage often find it hard to see any good in their husbands, yet usually, this is partly where the problem lies: often what is missing is an attitude of gratitude. Gratitude is one of the mysterious blessings from Allah. He has promised that the more we are grateful, the more He will increase us, and if we are ungrateful, His punishment is severe. How true this is in practical application. The more we are grateful to others, the more we get in return; if we discount what others do for us, they tend to stop.

Complete the following table by reflecting on all the things you are grateful for in your husband. Give it some time. At first, you may struggle to think of anything, but *keep writing until you fill the page!*

	e.g. He always brings me treats when I am poorly.
1	
2	
3	
4	
5	
6	
7	
8	
9	
10	

Exercise 3.3 Thank You

Now that you have completed the previous worksheet, write the list out again as a Thank You List for your husband. So, if in the previous exercise you wrote that you are grateful that he is a generous person, write: 'Thank you for being so generous.' You can use these Thank You's to brighten each day by saying it to him or even sending him a text message when he's not around.

I appreciate that... Thank you for... It means so much to me that... I love the fact that...

	e.g. It means so much to me that you clear the kitchen up in the evenings.
1	
2	
3	
4	
5	
6	
7	
8	
9	
10	

Exercise 3.4 The Five Love Languages of Receiving Love

The five love languages are:

1. Words of Affirmation
2. Acts of Service
3. Gifts
4. Quality Time
5. Physical Touch

On the following table, reflect on the languages that your husband uses to show his love to you, and the language that you prefer him to use. Also, reflect on the language that he uses which *doesn't* mean a lot to you—acknowledge that this too is a language of love!

THE LOVE LANGUAGE HE USES TO SHOW HIS LOVE TO ME	THE LOVE LANGUAGE I WANT HIM TO USE
(Receive graciously)	(Express your desires)
e.g. Acts of service: he hoovers the house	*e.g. Quality time: watch a movie together*

THIS LOVE LANGUAGE IS NOT THAT IMPORTANT TO ME
(Receive graciously)
e.g. Gifts: when he gets me flowers

The Four Traits of a Cherished Muslimah Workbook

Exercise 3.5 Receiving With Gratitude

Over the next few days, make a note of all the opportunities you have had to receive love, and make a note of how you received them with gratitude.

	WHAT DID I RECEIVE?	HOW DID I RECEIVE IT?
	e.g. My husband made me a cup of tea.	*I love it when you make me tea, thank you!*
1		
2		
3		
4		
5		
6		
7		
8		
9		
10		

Exercise 3.6 Receiving Graciously

How & Why Do I Miss Out?

Often we miss out on receiving love. Consider where you may be missing out and ask yourself why you miss out—what is your intention for missing an intimate connection? What do you want instead?

WORDS OF AFFIRMATION	
ACTS OF SERVICE	
GIFTS	
QUALITY TIME	
PHYSICAL TOUCH	

Exercise 3.7 Let Him Know Which Language You Prefer

Make a point of letting your husband know what your preferred love language is. Remember, you are simply expressing your desires—don't try to force him, or make him feel bad. Just let him know, and let this week be all about receiving well and expressing gratitude.

HOW I LET HIM KNOW	HOW HE RESPONDED

Exercise 3.8 Prayerful Gratitude

In this chapter, you have established your gratitude habit by taking stock of your blessings and thanking Allah for them, and all the good that you see in your husband and thanking him for what you appreciate in him. You have learnt how love can be expressed in different ways and seen how your husband expresses his love to you—being mindful of this ensures that you don't miss out on any acts of love that are coming from him. Remember, the more grateful you are, the more your blessings will increase. And again, it's time to pray for it! Call upon Allah with His names of love, generosity and provision. Revisit all of your intentions and goals for this habit and turn them into prayers.

GOALS & INTENTIONS	MY PRAYERS
GRATITUDE FOR BEING ME	
GRATITUDE TOWARDS HUSBAND	
LOVE LANGUAGES	
RECEIVING GRACIOUSLY	

4. Self-Care

Be like the rose in her self-care:
her thorns protect her growth and well-being.

Recommended Reading Point: The Four Traits of a Cherished Muslimah:
Chapter 5 - Self-Care

How to 'self-care'

One of the biggest obstacles to us women looking after ourselves is that we don't know how to do it. I once coached a lady who sent me a text message when she was about to take a timeout for 15 minutes, asking 'What exactly do I do when I do nothing for 15 minutes?' The difference between a relaxed, rested woman and a 'frazzled Franny'[3] is the difference between a wilted rose and one that is growing in the ground. You choose which one you want to be!

The Divine Names for Self-Care

When you cultivate the habit of self-care by connecting to Allah through His names, you acknowledge that He is the most merciful, caring and loving. You submit to His perfection and focus on looking after yourself, despite your weaknesses and flaws. You admit when you need to rest, and give your body its rights, acknowledging all your striving, and giving yourself respite for it. You nourish yourself through the gifts He has given you, and constantly praise Him while you look after yourself. When establishing your self-care habit, connect to Allah through His names of care, mercy and love, by putting them into practice/submitting to them, and call upon Him with them when you pray to Him.

SELF-CARE	
ALLAH (1)	The one who unites all the attributes of divinity
AR-RAHMĀN (2)	The merciful, without comparison
AR-RAHĪM (3)	The always merciful
AL-QUDŪS (5)	The flawless, transcends every attribute of perfection
AS-SALĀM (6)	He who is perfect, flawless, free from any insufficiency
AL-WAHĀB (17)	The bestower of gifts
AL-ADL (30)	He who is just in rulings and proportions
ASH-SHAKŪR (36)	He who gives more than one deserves
AL-WADŪD (48)	He who loves unconditionally
AL-WAKĪL (53)	He who takes responsibility for you
AL-WALĪ (56)	He who will stand for the believer
AL-MUQSIT (86)	The just in equity and fairness
AL-MUGHNĪ (89)	He who enriches you

Exercise 4.1 My Self-Care List

Start by making three lists on the following table: one with things that make you feel good, such as exercising, and decluttering; one with things that are fun, such as going to visit a friend for a coffee or starting a new course/hobby, and the last one with things that make you feel relaxed, like taking a nap, or taking a bubble bath. Then choose at least one thing (preferably more), and do some self-care every day!

Ask yourself, 'how do I feel?' and 'what do I want?'

Laura Doyle

	FEEL GOOD	**FUN**	**RELAXING**
	e.g. Exercising, decluttering, etc.	*e.g. Visit a friend for a coffee, starting a new course/hobby, etc.*	*e.g. Taking a nap, taking a bubble bath, etc.*
1			
2			
3			
4			
5			
6			
7			
8			
9			
10			

Exercise 4.2 Self-Care Overcoming Obstacles

The time will come when, with elation you will greet yourself arriving at your own door,
in your own mirror and each will smile at the other's welcome

Derek Walcott

Some women have neglected themselves for so long that they feel a sense of disconnect from their own selves. If they try to self-care, they don't know where to start. If you ask them what they want, they don't know! The good news is that when you finally start looking after yourself and speaking for yourself, you reconnect with how you are feeling, what you want, and what your limits, values and needs are. Some women feel like they are finally getting to know themselves. Fill in this table by reflecting on the obstacles that get in the way of your self-care, and possible solutions to overcome them.

WHAT I WANT TO DO	OBSTACLE	SOLUTION
e.g. Go to the gym	*e.g. Not feeling motivated*	*e.g. Reminding myself that it is to strengthen my body and mind. Calling upon Allah, Al-Aziz, to give me strength.*

The Four Traits of a Cherished Muslimah Workbook

Exercise 4.3 Prayerful Self-Care

In this chapter, you have looked at establishing a self-care habit and overcoming any obstacles in doing so. Reflect on why it is so important to have self-care in your life and ask Allah to give you the ability to ground you in a solid foundation of looking after yourself. Revisit all of your intentions and goals for this habit and turn them into prayers. Use these prayers to ask Allah daily, by His nurturing and caring names, with full conviction that every prayer is answered.

GOALS & INTENTIONS	MY PRAYERS
REGULAR SELF-CARE	
OVERCOMING SELF-CARE OBSTACLES	

WISDOM

5. Communication

Wisdom

5. Communication

*Be like the iris in her communication:
flexible and creative with her words.*

*Recommended Reading Point: The Four Traits of a Cherished Muslimah:
Introduction to Wisdom (page 135) & Chapter 8 – Communication*

Communication is all about getting your point across and conveying your truth to others. It isn't possible to do this unless:

1) you actually inform the other person

2) you inform them in a way that gets the desired message to them.

When you cultivate a healthy communication habit, you make a conscious effort to choose the best language to convey your meaning.

Words are powerful. We can make others happy, angry or even fall in love with us. This habit is about choosing the words that give you the results that you desire. The following six 'sentence starters' are one of the most effective ways of getting your point across, and we will be focusing on them whilst developing the communication habit. Apart from the last one (making requests) each sentence starter is about you—what you want, what you feel and what your limits, values and needs are.

The Divine Names for Communication

When you cultivate the habit of communication by connecting to Allah through His names, you acknowledge that He is the one with knowledge of all things, the all-seeing and all-hearing, knowing that He is the one who makes things happen or delays things and takes account of everything. You reflect and ponder upon your situation and inform others wisely and truthfully, knowing that through Him, you will get the perfect results. When establishing your communication habit, connect to Allah through His names of divine knowledge and wisdom, by putting them into practice/submitting to them, and call upon Him with them when you pray to Him.

COMMUNICATION	
ALLAH (1)	The one who unites all the attributes of divinity
AL-MU'MIN (7)	He who has all the knowledge about Him
AL-FATĀH (19)	The exposer/opener of truth
AL-ALĪM (20)	He who knows everything
AS-SAMĪ (27)	The all-hearing
AL-BASĪR (28)	The all-seeing
AL-LATĪF (31)	The subtle, He who leads one onto an unexpected path
AL-KHABĪR (32)	The one who informs to ponder and reflect
AR-RAQĪB (44)	He who is observing at all times
AL-HAKĪM (47)	The wise
AL-HAQQ (52)	The truth
AN-NŪR (93)	The light (of guidance)
AL-HĀDI (94)	The guide (to the light)

Exercise 5.1 Undeniable Truths

By the declining day! Verily, man is a state of loss,
Except those who exhort one another to truth and exhort one another to patience.

Al-Asr (103)

I remember the time I was sat in the Dower House for my NLP Master Practitioner training with my late teacher, Paul Jacobs. My task was to build rapport with him using undeniable truths, by simply talking about facts. Here's how it went:

Me: So, we are sat here in the training room.

(Paul nodded his head in agreement)

Me: *(pointing to the window)* And it's a lovely day outside.

Paul: *(shaking his head)* No, how do you know that I don't have hayfever? It might not be a lovely day for me.

Me: *(correcting myself)* The sun is shining outside.

(Paul nodded his head in agreement)

Me: *(pointing to Paul's beloved brown leather sandals)* And you are wearing your comfortable sandals.

Paul: *(shaking his head)* No, how do you know they are comfortable? They may have given me a blister.

Me: *(correcting myself)* And you are wearing your brown sandals.

(Paul nodded his head in agreement)

Think of a recent challenging conversation you have had with your husband. How do you typically say things? Do you state undeniable truths or are your statements open to interpretation? Do you get him nodding his head in agreement, or does he shake his head and not accept your 'version of events'?

The Four Traits of a Cherished Muslimah Workbook

Exercise 5.2 How Not to Express Desires

Recommended Reading Point: The Four Traits of a Cherished Muslimah:
Expressing Desires (page 144)

A lot of ladies think they are expressing desires when they are actually not. When you express your desires, you are simply expressing what you want instead of:

1. Asking him (that's a request, not a desire)
2. Expressing your desires and expecting them to be fulfilled
3. Speaking for 'we' instead of 'me'
4. Asking him if 'he' wants it
5. Explaining and justifying your desires
6. Making him guess
7. Instructing him
8. Using other men as a comparison

Reflect on the unhealthy habits you may currently have when expressing desires. What stops you from directly asking?

Exercise 5.3 Ten Desires off the Top of Your Head

Think of all the things that you desire and write them down. These don't have to be realistic desires—they can be as wishful as you want! Also, reflect on how you normally express your desires. Do you express them by saying 'I want' or by saying something else?

	I WANT…	HOW I NORMALLY EXPRESS IT
	e.g. I want to do something nice for our anniversary.	*We've not been anywhere nice in ages.*
1		
2		
3		
4		
5		
6		
7		
8		
9		
10		

Exercise 5.4 Expressing Feelings – The 'I Feel' Camouflage

Recommended Reading Point: The Four Traits of a Cherished Muslimah: Expressing Feelings (page 147)

It's quite eye-opening when I coach ladies and get them to use the 'I feel' sentence starter. It usually goes something like this:

- I feel that you should help me more around the house.
- I feel that I need you to prioritise our relationship.
- I feel ignored by you.

And none of the sentences are actually talking about how they are feeling!

When we express our feelings, we are expressing our emotional state and getting in touch with what's going on inside *us*. In the previous three examples, the focus of the communication is on the other person rather than oneself. In each of the examples, a value or belief is being expressed as opposed to how one is feeling, but the 'I feel' at the beginning of the sentence is camouflaging the value or belief.

So, using the same examples you could say:

- I feel overwhelmed with my workload.
- I feel undervalued and unimportant.
- I feel lonely.

In this exercise, reflect on a few situations that have caused you to feel a particular way. Reflect on what is happening and how it makes you feel:

WHEN THIS HAPPENS	I FEEL
e.g. When my husband calls me a 'dope' when I make a mistake.	*I feel hurt and belittled.*

Exercise 5.5 Expressing Limitations - I Can't... But I Can, Really!

Recommended Reading Point: The Four Traits of a Cherished Muslimah: Expressing Limitations (page 151)

And to be of those who believe and exhort one another to perseverance and exhort one another to compassion. Those are the companions of the right.

Al-Balad (90:17-18)

When you say I can't (or I can), you are letting your husband know that you're going to stay within your limits.

Definition of 'can':

- To be able to
- To have the ability to

And so, it's very important to actually mean what you say. If you say you can't do something, then don't.

Reflect on three times when you have had to express your limitations and how you have said it. Could you have said it more effectively?

I HAD TO EXPRESS MY LIMITS WHEN	HOW I SAID IT	HOW I COULD HAVE SAID IT BETTER
My husband asked me if I could supervise builders on a day I was really busy with work.	You know I'm busy on that day, why would you ask such a thing?	I can't do it on that particular day, but I could do it another day.

Exercise 5.6 My Values

Recommended Reading Point: The Four Traits of a Cherished Muslimah: Expressing Your Values (page 153)

Values are things that are important to us. They help us to decide what is good or bad, and what is right or wrong. When our values are not honoured (by ourselves or others) we react from unhealthy places of fear, anger and resentment. What values do you have about marriage?

	IT'S IMPORTANT TO ME THAT…
	e.g. I rest when I am tired
1	
2	
3	
4	
5	
6	
7	
8	
9	
10	

Making Requests

Recommended Reading Point: The Four Traits of a Cherished Muslimah: Undeniable Truths (page 141)

When you make requests, you are hoping for a change. The best way to encourage change is to first get rapport with the other person and one of the best ways to do that is to use undeniable truths (see *The Four Traits of a Cherished Muslimah,* page 141). In this exercise, we will look at how to use undeniable truths effectively when making requests using the S-E-S-E formula.

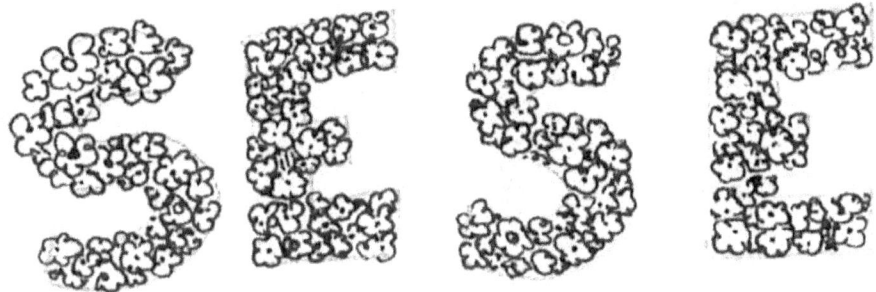

Exercise 5.7 Situation – Effect – Suggestion – Effect

> *Invite to the way of your Lord with wisdom and beautiful instruction; and reason with them in ways that are best: for your Lord knows best who have strayed from His path, and who receive guidance.*
>
> *An-Nahl (16:125)*

The S-E-S-E formula is very effective when making requests. The aim is to get rapport with your husband before making a request. Address two situations in your marriage that you would like to change. Reflect on how you would use the Situation - Effect - Suggestion - Effect formula to address them. Once you have done this, reflect on how this would be different from your normal way of doing things. Would it make a difference? If so, how?

SITUATION	EFFECT	SUGGESTION	EFFECT
What is happening	The effect the situation is having on you and your relationship	State desire/make request	The effect the suggestion will have on you and your relationship
e.g. My husband is coming home from work extremely late.	*We don't get time to spend together. I am feeling really lonely.*	*I would appreciate it if you could come home earlier.*	*You wouldn't be so exhausted, and we could spend time together.*

CONSIDER HOW YOU USUALLY MAKE REQUESTS. WHAT'S THE DIFFERENCE?

Exercise 5.8 Body Language

Recommended Reading Point: The Four Traits of a Cherished Muslimah: Body Language (page 160)

> *It is due to mercy from Allah that you deal with them gently, and had you been rough, hard hearted, they would certainly have dispersed from around you; so pardon them, and ask for forgiveness for them, and consult them in the affair; and when you have decided, then place your trust in Allah; surely Allah loves those who trust.*
>
> *Al-Imran (3:159)*

Don't forget that our bodies are responding internally to our values, beliefs, memories and decisions, and if these are not positive, then our body language will never be. We will discuss this further in Chapter 6, Respecting Others. It doesn't matter how polite your words are; if you are saying it in a harsh voice or using disapproving expressions, it's likely that your words won't help you attain your desired outcome.

> *The meaning of your communication is the response you get.*
>
> *NLP Presupposition*

Reflect here on what your body, voice and words are saying when you communicate. Are they all in harmony with each other? Are they singing the same song? Are they telling the same story? Are they all gentle and respectful?

	BODY	VOICE	WORDS
CURRENT WAY			
WHAT I COULD IMPROVE			

The Four Traits of a Cherished Muslimah Workbook

Exercise 5.9 The 'Big Stuff' vs the 'Small Stuff'

Recommended Reading Point: The Four Traits of a Cherished Muslimah: The Big Stuff vs The Small Stuff (page 161)

Part of communicating wisely is acknowledging that some things must be dealt with, and some things need to be let go of—perhaps even accepted. Often there are so many needs in the marital garden, that one does not know where to start. The best policy to apply at this time is 'Don't Sweat The Small Stuff'.[4]

In the inner circle, write all the things that you can't compromise on and in the outer circle, write all the things that you could compromise on. For the sake of harmony, try to be more generous of what you give from your outer circle, and for the sake of self-preservation, hold on to the things in the inner circle.

Exercise 5.10 My Wants vs My Needs

Recommended Reading Point: The Four Traits of a Cherished Muslimah:
Self Respect: Needs vs Wants (pages 240-244)

Whosoever of you sees an evil, let him change it with his hand; and if he is not able to do so, then [let him change it] with his tongue; and if he is not able to do so, then with his heart—and that is the weakest of faith.

Muslim (49)

Having healthy boundaries means that you can differentiate between wants and needs, and then communicate them clearly to others. Although establishing boundaries is a part of the self-respect habit, this exercise is included here as our needs must be communicated so that others are aware of them; a bit like a 'No Trespassing' sign in your garden.

I once coached a lady who didn't recognise the difference between her wants and her needs. She would insist on the things she wanted with so much firmness but didn't notice her needs were going unmet. Let's use this opportunity to differentiate between the two. Your wants are desires that you would like but *can* live without. Needs are necessities, and you should do whatever it takes to get them met.

The Four Traits of a Cherished Muslimah Workbook

MY WANTS	WHAT WOULD HAPPEN IF I DIDN'T GET THEM?	MY NEEDS	WHAT WOULD HAPPEN IF I DIDN'T GET THEM?	HOW TO GET MY NEEDS MET
A volume of books	*Nothing. I would just have to wait till I got them.*	*If I haven't had enough sleep, I need to sleep!*	*I would be unable to function, grouchy, grumpy….*	*Let everyone know I am going to bed.*

Exercise 5.11 Express Yourself

Complete the worksheet using three typical situations that you have problems with and express yourself using only the following five sentence starters. Reflect on how different these conversations would flow if you started using these sentence starters instead of the first thing that comes to mind.

SITUATION	DESIRES 'I WANT'	FEELINGS 'I FEEL'	LIMITATIONS 'I CAN'T'	VALUES 'IT'S IMPORTANT TO ME THAT...'	NEEDS 'I NEED'
e.g. Woken up with a cold	I want to take it easy today	I feel sick	I can't cook today	It's important to me that I rest when I'm sick	I need to sleep till I feel better
1					
2					
3					

The Four Traits of a Cherished Muslimah Workbook

Exercise 5.12 An Inner Place of Refuge

I only complain of my grief and sorrow to Allah.

Yusuf (12:86)

Sometimes, despite our very best efforts and prayers, things don't go the way that we want. At times like these, it's a great blessing to be able to share the pain with one's spouse. Yet sometimes the pain is unfortunately the result of one's spouse. It is essential that we have our own inner place of refuge and enough resources to self-soothe if we find ourselves in this situation.

Reflect on what you can do to make yourself feel better at times when it feels like you can't turn to your spouse for comfort or support. There are some self-soothing suggestions on page 167 of *The Four Traits of a Cherished Muslimah* to help you. Look and reach out for other areas of support. Sometimes we have more support around us, and within us, than we realise.

Exercise 5.13 Prayerful Communication

O my Lord! expand me my breast; Ease my task for me;
And remove the impediment from my speech, So they may understand what I say.

Ta-ha (20:25-28)

In this chapter, you have looked at how to express desires, feelings, limits and values and how to use them in your conversations. When making requests, it is easier to communicate when you have rapport and when your body language is also communicating the same message! You have also looked at differentiating between the big stuff and the small stuff—no one is perfect, and we all have our flaws, and so identifying what matters in your marriage is an essential habit to cultivate. Finally, you reflected on ways you can self-soothe when no matter how much you communicate, things are still difficult. Revisit all of your intentions and goals for this habit and turn them into prayers, invoking Allah by His names for guidance and divine gifts, knowing that He is Al-Karīm and will give us what we need before we even ask for it.

GOALS & INTENTIONS	MY PRAYERS
SENTENCE STARTERS	
MAKING REQUESTS WITH S-E-S-E	
BODY LANGUAGE	
BIG STUFF VS SMALL STUFF	
MY INNER PLACE OF REFUGE	

JUSTICE

6. Respecting Others

Justice

6. Respecting Others

Be like the gladiolus when respecting others:
ensuring that her words don't cause anyone undue harm.

Recommended Reading Point: The Four Traits of a Cherished Muslimah:
Introduction to Justice (page 205) & Chapter 11 - Respecting Others

Respecting others requires us to step out of our world and into someone else's. When we respect our husbands, we acknowledge that they are their own person. They have their own inner garden and they have their own growth and roots and require their own nourishment.

> *Love one another, but make not a bond of love:*
> *Let it rather be a moving sea between the shores of your souls.*
> *Fill each other's cup but drink not from one cup.*
> *Give one another of your bread but eat not from the same loaf.*
> *Sing and dance together and be joyous, but let each one of you be alone,*
> *Even as the strings of the lute are alone though they quiver with the same music.*
> *Give your hearts, but not into each other's keeping.*
> *For only the hand of Life can contain your hearts.*
> *And stand together yet not too near together:*
> *For the pillars of the temple stand apart,*
> *And the oak tree and the cypress grow not in each other's shadow.*
>
> *Kahlil Gibran*

When we are respectful, we acknowledge that we are all different yet can be together. When you accept your husband for who he is, and not who you *want* him to be, you can cultivate a joint garden where you both grow. By upholding both of your boundaries, your marriage will be nourished. Let's respect others by acknowledging each other's filtering processes, personality types and by taking a closer look at what it really means to respect one another.

The Divine Names for Respecting Others

When you cultivate the habit of respecting others by connecting to Allah through His names, you acknowledge that He is the judge, and you ensure that all of your dealings with others are all according to His law. You bring into practice His names of honour by honouring others. You know He will stand for you, protect you and be a witness for you and so armed with this power, His power, you know you can be respectful no matter what situation you find yourself in. When establishing the habit of respecting others, connect to Allah through His names of justice, honour and truth, by putting them into practice/submitting to them, and call upon Him with them when you pray to Him.

RESPECTING OTHERS	
ALLAH (1)	The one who unites all the attributes of divinity
AL-MUTAKABBIR (11)	He who is elevated above all
AR-RĀFI (24)	He who raises up
AL-MU'IZ (25)	The giver of honour
AL-MUDHIL (26)	The taker of honour
AL-HAKAM (29)	The judge
AL-ADL (30)	He who is just in rulings and proportions
AL-HALĪM (33)	He who forgives when angry, even if one is deserving of it
ASH-SHAHĪD (51)	The witness
AL-HAQQ (52)	The truth
AL-AFŪ' (82)	He who forgives and forgets
AL-MUQSIT (86)	The just in equity and fairness
AL-MĀNI (90)	The protector, creates causes for protection, the powerful withholder

Justice

Exercise 6.1 Same Event, Different Response

The purpose of this exercise is to develop an awareness that all our experiences go through a filtering process which causes us to behave differently. Think of an event that has occurred in the past where you and your spouse have had different reactions and responses. Consider the different filters (values, beliefs, decisions and memories) that led to these two different responses.

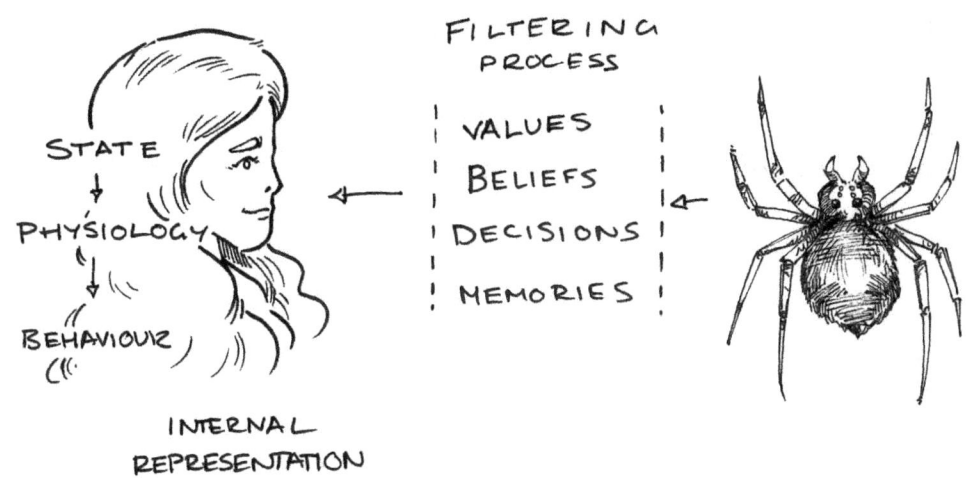

EVENT	
YOUR RESPONSE	**YOUR HUSBAND'S RESPONSE**
YOUR FILTERS	**YOUR HUSBAND'S FILTERS**

The Four Traits of a Cherished Muslimah Workbook

Exercise 6.2 Identify Your Personality Type

The Myers-Briggs type indicator gives us a useful way of sorting different 'personality types' and gives each person an indication of how they function *innately* in terms of sensing, intuition, feeling, and thinking. Interestingly, this questionnaire was designed and developed by mother and daughter Katherine Briggs and Isabel Myers, based on the archetypal concepts of Carl Jung, to determine how people work the best, doing what they do the best.

You can take the MBTI Personality Test here: http://www.humanmetrics.com/cgi-win/JTypes2.asp

Once you have identified your personality type, record it here, along with the percentages of each category of introversion/extroversion, sensing/intuition, thinking/feeling and judging/perception. You may also choose to write other bits of information that you have found to be true for your personality type. Did anything surprise you?

Exercise 6.3 Respect

Complete the worksheet to see how respectful you are. Awareness of where you can improve will help you to form the habit of respect.

	HOLDING HIM IN HIGH REGARD	✓
1	You have a good opinion of him and see him as being worthy of respect.	
2	You honour his way of doing things and don't automatically assume that your way is best. When he does something in his way, you respect it and don't redo what he does due to the notion that your way is better.	
3	You honour the choices he makes in his life without criticism, disapproval and without trying to control.	
4	You speak highly of him in front of others.	
5	You forgive him when he makes mistakes.	
6	You lead by example instead of trying to impress your views on him.	
	BEING NICE, NOT NASTY	✓
7	You speak to him with respect and refrain from insults.	
8	You refrain from using sarcasm.	
9	You refrain from laughing at, mocking or belittling him.	
10	You ensure that you look at him respectfully and refrain from disapproving expressions.	
11	You do not withhold sexual intimacy as a way to control or punish him.	
	LISTENING	✓
12	You listen to his dreams and thoughts.	
13	You don't minimise or discount what he says.	
14	You allow him to speak for himself and not on his behalf.	
15	You refrain from interrupting when he is speaking.	

Exercise 6.4 Why Do I Disrespect?

Following on from the previous exercise, look at the ways that you disrespect your husband, and reflect on the effects and pay-offs you get when you do and what a better way would be. Sometimes we do things out of habit, or sometimes because we have a different pay-off, such as feeling in control, or even feeling superior.

HOW I DISRESPECT	EFFECTS ON MARRIAGE	PAY-OFFS/ BENEFITS FOR ME	A BETTER WAY OF DOING IT
e.g. I disapprove of him going to the gym so often.	*He feels upset with me and goes anyway.*	*He gets to know how I'm feeling.*	*Tell him I want to spend more time with him.*

Exercise 6.5 Control – Wanting Him to Do Things My Way

Reflect on why you want your husband to do things your way and how your behaviour is interpreted. What is the alternative?

AREA OF CONTROL	WHY I CONTROL	THE MESSAGE I SEND OUT IS	THE ALTERNATIVE
1. Things you want him to do for you – how, when, where			
2. His health			
3. His appearance			
4. His career			
5. His religion			
6. What he does to relax			
7. How he manages his time			
8. How he manages his budget			
9. Withdrawing physically/withholding intimacy			
10. Using tears to manipulate			
11. Using your body/lingerie to persuade him to be intimate (as opposed to simply seduce)			
12. Using pressure from your family to change him			

Exercise 6.6 Am I Controlling My Own Life?

In the table below, reflect on the areas you control in your own life, and that of your husband's. Are you exercising enough self-control in your own life or are you spending all your time and energy trying to control his? If you don't maintain control over the areas of your own life, then reflect on how you will benefit from doing so. Similarly, if you try to control areas of your husband's life, consider how things would be different if you stopped.

AREA OF CONTROL	HOW DO I EXERCISE SELF-CONTROL IN MY OWN LIFE?	HOW DO I CONTROL MY HUSBAND'S LIFE?	HOW WOULD THINGS BE DIFFERENT IF I FOCUSED ON MY LIFE AND NOT HIS?
1. Health			
2. Appearance			
3. Running one's home/business			
4. Fulfilling one's guardianship role			
5. Spare time			
6. Time management			
7. Negative emotions and anger			
8. Sexual availability			
9. Money/budget			

Exercise 6.7 Prayerful Apologising

Marital conflicts and disagreements can be very painful as often both parties believe with full conviction that they have been mistreated and feel misunderstood. Yet unfortunately, we frequently forget our part in the conflict, and how we have fanned the flames of discord. There is a hilarious episode of the comedy *Everybody Loves Raymond* where both the husband and wife recount the same story to different family members, making themselves look like angels and the other to be a monster. Same event, totally different perceptions!

If you find yourself being disrespectful, here's what to do:

1. Start observing yourself and noticing your actions and words.
2. When you find yourself being inadvertently disrespectful, apologise to your husband as soon as you can.
3. Privately, ask Allah for forgiveness and help. Repent to Him and ask Him to forgive you and make an intention to not do it again. Ask Him for the ability and wisdom to treat all of His slaves with respect and to give you balance in the traits that are imbalanced.
4. Start over.

Think of the most recent incident of when you disrespected your husband, and reflect on how you will start over:

Exercise 6.8 Apologising Using the 5 Languages of Apology

Sometimes a simple 'I'm sorry' isn't enough. Reflect below on how you can use the Languages of Apology to make a more effective and sincere apology:[5]

EXPRESSING REGRET Saying the words 'I'm sorry'	*I'm sorry that I invited guests over tomorrow when I know that you are busy.*
ACCEPTING RESPONSIBILITY Accepting responsibility for being disrespectful	*I should have checked with you first.*
MAKING RESTITUTION Moving forward by doing things right	*I will ring them and tell them that we have other plans that I overlooked.*
GENUINELY REPENTING Not repeating the mistake again	*I will make sure I check with you next time before I arrange plans that affect you.*
REQUESTING FORGIVENESS	*Can you forgive me?*

Exercise 6.9 Pressing the Reset Button

Recommended Reading Point: The Four Traits of a Cherished Muslimah: A New Respectful You (page 231)

I always recommend pressing the Reset Button when disrespectful habits start to become the norm and starting over by apologising, making a new intention, letting your husband know of it, and starting afresh in a respectful way.

HOW I RESET THE RELATIONSHIP

HOW MY HUSBAND REACTED

STEPS I CAN TAKE TO SELF-SOOTHE

Exercise 6.10 Prayerful Respect

This habit is all about respecting others. Mutual respect is essential in any relationship, but perhaps even more so in a marriage as it is a place where two separate and different lives come together to grow harmoniously.

To establish this habit, you have looked at how the same event can have a different impact on both you and your spouse, and how your personality type influences your behaviour. You have also looked at the different ways to respect (and disrespect!)—knowing this can help you identify what is your business and what is not. Finally, you looked at the importance of effective apologising and pressing the Reset Button to re-establish a respectful culture in your marriage. Revisit all of your intentions and goals for this chapter and turn them into prayers, calling upon Allah with His names of honour and justice.

GOALS & INTENTIONS	MY PRAYERS
MY PERSONALITY TYPE	
RESPECTFUL BEHAVIOUR	
CONTROL	
APOLOGISING	
PRESSING THE RESET BUTTON	

Nourishment

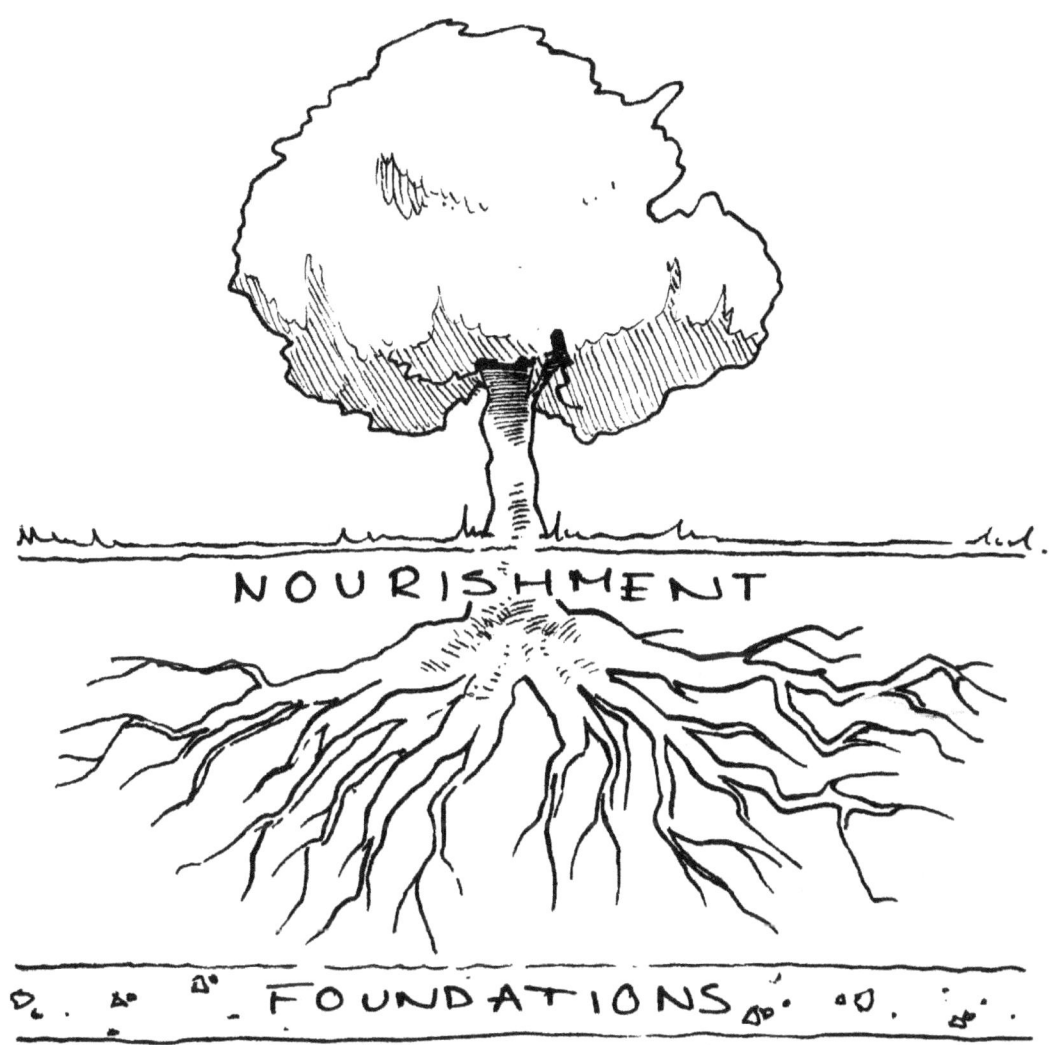

Nourishment

Establishing a healthy foundation with the four traits brings about balance in our lives and opens us up to receive love; it helps us to be a more relaxed, loving person and gives us the ability to choose the right words for effective communication. Most importantly, it helps us to understand what it means to respect another person. Once these are established, we can then provide our gardens with *nourishment* by adding even more leadership, love, wisdom and justice, resulting in healthy and flourishing growth.

Nourishment through the four traits gives you ownership of your guardianship roles, nurtures the marriage by giving love, brings peace through healing and the knowledge that time plays a big part in the growth of relationships and provides protection by healthy boundaries. A nourished marriage provides balance through clarity; both husband and wife are clear on what their roles are in their unique working balance so that breadwinning, parenting and housekeeping become rewarding experiences instead of burdens. When the roles and responsibilities of marriage are balanced and fair, you can embrace your duties, creating a deeper connection with your spouse, your children, your home and your career, if you have one.

Through nourishment, you can become a master delegator and if you can't do something, you can find someone who can. Your energy levels are regularly recharged through love and security so that you can effectively manage your time, energy and money. Your marriage becomes a colourful blend of your and your husband's strengths and weaknesses. A nourished life provides healing so that instead of being consumed by incidents and memories from the past, you can learn many lessons through the experiences of life and embrace each day at a time. Through nourishing boundaries, instead of feeling like a doormat or a woman who does too much, you feel strong and confident, and powerful beyond measure.

In the next section of the workbook, we will look at how to establish the remaining six habits in your life, starting with Guardianship.

LEADERSHIP	**LOVE**
7. Guardianship	*8. Giving Love*

WISDOM	**JUSTICE**
9. Healing *10. Time*	*11. Self-Respect* *12. Self-Discipline*

LEADERSHIP

7. Guardianship

Leadership

7. Guardianship

*Be like the lily in her guardianship:
procreating and nurturing in harmony with the masculine.*

*Recommended Reading Point: The Four Traits of a Cherished Muslimah:
Chapter 3 – Guardianship*

The guardianship habit looks at how you can embrace your roles as a guardian of your husband's home and your children, and your husband's role as the guardian of the family.

The lily proudly boasts her life-giving nature and fertility. Be proud of being a woman and to be connected to Allah's mercy (Arabic: *rahmah*) through the very womb (Arabic: *rahm*) which He has given you, that distinguishes you so beautifully from your husband. Show your gratitude for the way He fashioned you by being a mercy to all those around you, including yourself.

Allah has made the man financially responsible for his family, and it is helpful to have a monthly budget for the house and home to calculate exactly how much money it takes for a woman to run her home and meet the needs of herself and her children.

The guardianship habit looks at creating a unique working balance in your marriage, by identifying what your family's needs are and discussing the best ways to get them met. You and your husband may both have a career, or perhaps only one of you do. A unique working balance means both of you carry and support each other in a way that works best for you.

A healthy guardianship habit means that you embrace your roles as a homemaker and mother by delegating your roles in a way that ensures all members of the family have a fair workload. It also means that you establish being the joint 'captain of the ship' and you raise your children with your husband in a parenting partnership.

The Divine Names for Guardianship

When you cultivate the habit of guardianship by connecting to Allah through His names, you ensure that you are as merciful and fair as you can be, looking after the needs and wants of those in your charge. You are innovative, creating and fashioning solutions unique for your family, giving and nourishing them within your means and abilities. You bring life to your home through His power and as He looks after all of your needs, you in turn look after the needs of others, using your intuition to fulfil the needs of those under your care. When establishing the habit of guardianship, connect to Allah through His names of care, compassion and nourishment, by putting them into practice/submitting to them, and call upon Him with them when you pray to Him.

GUARDIANSHIP	
ALLAH (1)	The one who unites all the attributes of divinity
AR-RAHMĀN (2)	The merciful, without comparison
AR-RAHĪM (3)	The always merciful
AL-MUHAYMIN (8)	He who encompasses needs/wants
AL-BĀRI (13)	The producer, without any previous example
AL-MUSAWWIR (14)	The fashioner
AR-RAZZĀQ (18)	The giver, provider
AL-MUQĪT (40)	The maintainer and nourisher of food and knowledge
AL-WADŪD (48)	He who loves unconditionally
AL-WAKĪL (53)	He who takes responsibility for you
AL-WALĪ (56)	He who will stand for the believer
AL-MUHYI (61)	The giver of life
AL-MUMĪT (62)	The taker of life

Exercise 7.1 Make a Spending Plan

As a guardian of your home and children, you will benefit from having autonomy on where and when you will spend your money. If you don't have this, or you need more financial support from your husband in order to effectively fulfil your guardianship roles, then it may be helpful to create a spending plan and discuss it with your husband.

Make a realistic, generous and thorough spending plan for yourself.

1. Write down everything you anticipate you'll need for a month and when in doubt, allow yourself slightly more instead of less, to make sure you'll have enough.
2. Include all the things you normally buy, including the groceries and spending money for yourself.
3. If you have children, include their expenses in your plan, fees for extra classes, toys, clothes, school trips, and their entertainment.
4. Discuss this plan with your husband and come to an agreement on how these financial needs can be met.

My monthly spending plan

OUTGOINGS	£
TOTAL	
MONTHLY BUDGET	

Exercise 7.2 What Mothers Do, When It Looks Like Nothing

I love the title of this book by Naomi Stadlen! How many women sit around and wonder how unproductive their days have been when all they have done is *sit at home and do the mundane*. It is easy to feel fed up and wonder what the point is behind housework.

Take a closer look at what you do, and you will find that as mothers and homemakers, we fulfil pretty amazing tasks! Give yourself credit for all that you do, and thank Allah for giving you the opportunity to do so many acts of goodness on a daily basis, and this will help you to embrace the habit of guardianship.

What did I do today?

Take a moment to reflect on all the things you have done today, and what is important about each task. You will find that there are many positive intentions behind each task.

WHAT DID I DO TODAY?	WHAT IS IMPORTANT ABOUT THAT?
e.g. I went grocery shopping	*To provide healthy food for my family*

Exercise 7.3 Your Couple's Unique Working Balance

What would the Prophet ﷺ do when he entered his house? He would busy himself with serving his family, then when (the time for) prayer was due he would stand (to go) for it.

Tirmidhi (2489)

Finding your couple's unique working balance means balancing out your roles and responsibilities as a team. Today's couples are faced with challenges unique to them, not faced by the women of the past. Typically both spouses work and a woman usually drives as well, lightening the load for the man but increasing her duties. I remember the amount of prayers my father-in-law made for me to pass my driving test, and when I did (fifth time lucky!), he was delighted. He put his keys down and told us that his role of driving my mother-in-law around was over! Even a woman who doesn't work full-time is normally very busy out of the home and is not simply a stay-at-home mother. So how does a couple manage the workload? It just can't be the case that the husband goes to work and pays the bills and the wife does everything else while working herself, without any help or support from him.

Roles & Responsibilities

In this exercise, look at all of your roles as husband and wife, and see how you can both create a working balance where both of you share your workload fairly.

ROLE	YOUR UNIQUE WORKING BALANCE	
	YOU	HIM
e.g. Mum and dad's taxi	Afternoon school run and evening classes	Morning school run and weekend classes

Exercise 7.4 Are You A Happy Housewife?

How do you fare as the guardian of your home? Do you see it is a pleasurable and rewarding experience? In her book *Happy Housewives,* Darla Shine inspires and motivates women to find the glory in being a happy housewife by encouraging them to be grateful, stylish and healthy (both emotionally and physically). Complete this worksheet to see if you are a Happy Housewife:

ARE YOU A HAPPY HOUSEWIFE?	✓
You are grateful for your blessings every day.	
You are proud of being a housewife, and you see it as the most important job.	
You understand the importance of taking the time to raise your kids.	
You wear stylish clothes and look like a lady, and not 'mumsy' and 'homely'.	
You make your own health number 1 priority.	
Your marriage comes above your housewifely duties.	
You regularly pace yourself so you are not too exhausted for physical intimacy by the end of the day.	
Your home is a place of functionality, beauty, comfort and hygge.[6]	
You have simple routines which make the workload lighter.	
You accept responsibility to do the menial work in the home to create a sanctuary for the whole family.	
You express creativity through your cooking.	
You regularly cook simple and effective meals for your family so you have time for other things.	
You regularly meet and speak to your girlfriends – there is more to life than your home.	
You take time out for yourself – you have energy and drive to run the home.	

Role Delegation

Shall I teach you a thing which is better than what you have asked me? When you go to bed, say, 'Allahu Akbar' thirty-four times, and 'SubhanAllah' thirty-three times, and 'Alhamdulillah' thirty-three times for that is better for you both than a servant.

Bukhari (3705)

There is a beautiful narration of Sayyidina Ali, that his wife, Sayyida Fatimah (may Allah be pleased with her) the daughter of the Messenger of Allah ﷺ was suffering due to her difficult workload, and wanted to ask for a maid from her father ﷺ. Her father ﷺ instead guided her to a unique invocation: to recite 'Allahu Akbar' thirty-four times, 'SubhanAllah' thirty-three times, and 'Alhamdulillah' thirty-three times, and she was told that this would be *better for her than a servant!*

Once I was taking the clothes out of the tumble dryer and was so overworked and exhausted, I wanted to cry. I remembered the Tasbih Fatimah and started to recite it, saying: 'Oh Allah! I don't have a servant, but this tasbih is meant to be better, so I am reciting it! Help me Allah!' A few weeks later during a family meeting, the laundry was delegated three ways: one of my sons took the responsibility of the darks, I took the lights and another son took the towels and bathmats. Fast-forward a few months and now all of my children, including my 8-year-old daughter, are doing their own laundry! If that wasn't a blessing enough, my husband and my sons have all started financially contributing towards a cleaner who comes three times a week. I had not envisaged these outcomes when I had called upon Allah that day, totally overwhelmed.

Too much on your plate? Take your petition to Allah! I have found that whenever things have gotten hard to the point I can no longer bear it, the Tasbih Fatimah has saved me: either it has grounded me or made unexpected ways out for me.

The Four Traits of a Cherished Muslimah Workbook

Exercise 7.5 Role Delegation

In this exercise, start with reciting the Tasbih Fatimah, and then reflect on all the responsibilities you have as a homemaker and see how you can lighten your load by delegating/outsourcing.

RESPONSIBILITIES I HAVE	DELEGATE TO	OUTSOURCE TO	LEAVE IT ✓	DO IT MYSELF ✓
e.g. Ironing		Launderette		
e.g. Cooking on a busy Thursday	Eldest son			

Leadership

Exercise 7.6 Am I the Captain of My Ship?

It is important to remember that parents need to be in charge of their children, just like a captain is in charge of her ship. When no one is in charge, life is filled with debating, bargaining and arguing. When you let your children know that you are in charge and you make the rules, and you help them accept it and deal with it, they will respect your decisions and feel safe in them. See how you fare with being the captain of your ship:

	AM I THE CAPTAIN OF MY SHIP?	✓
1	I am the captain of the ship – I am in charge of my kids.	
2	I help my children deal with frustration.	
3	I give my children in fantasy what I can't give them in reality.	
4	I know when to support my children emotionally, and when to support them logically.	
5	I speak in my child's preferred love language.	
6	I take time out for my children. I make time. I find the time.	
7	I teach my children to be responsible, whilst not overburdening them.	
8	I teach my children to please Allah, whilst being considerate to themselves and others.	
9	I encourage my children to be proactive whilst pacing themselves.	
10	I encourage my children to progressively improve themselves whilst avoiding obsessive perfection.	
11	I teach my children to be competent by stepping out of their comfort zones, whilst staying within their endurance limits.	

Exercise 7.7 Dealing with Frustration

One of the most important things we can learn and also teach our children is how to deal with frustration. Reflect on how you deal with your frustration. Where did you learn that from? How does your child deal with frustration? Where did he/she learn that from? How do you currently deal with your child's frustration? How can you help your child deal with his/her frustration?

HOW DO YOU DEAL WITH YOUR FRUSTRATION? WHERE DID YOU LEARN THAT FROM? WHAT UNMET NEED DO YOU HAVE?	HOW DOES YOUR CHILD DEAL WITH FRUSTRATION? WHERE DID HE/SHE LEARN THAT FROM? WHAT UNMET NEED DO THEY HAVE?	HOW DO YOU CURRENTLY DEAL WITH YOUR CHILD'S FRUSTRATION?	HOW CAN YOU HELP YOUR CHILD DEAL WITH HIS/HER FRUSTRATION?

Exercise 7.8 Parenting Partnership

Look at the strengths and weaknesses of both you and your spouse. The areas you are stronger in are ideally the areas you can lead in your parenting partnership; the same applies to your husband. If either of you have certain weaknesses, look to see if you can help each other.

	PARENTING STRENGTHS	PARENTING WEAKNESSES	AREAS YOU CAN HELP ONE ANOTHER
YOU			
YOUR HUSBAND			

The Four Traits of a Cherished Muslimah Workbook

Exercise 7.9 Prayerful Guardianship

In this chapter, you have been establishing a healthy guardianship habit by identifying your and your husband's unique working balance in terms of finances, roles and responsibilities, and delegating appropriately. The guardianship habit involves embracing the highs and lows of motherhood and homemaking and being the captain of the ship when it comes to parenting. Revisit all of your intentions and goals for this habit and turn them into prayers, asking Allah, by His names of love, mercy and guardianship.

GOALS & INTENTIONS	MY PRAYERS
MY MARRIAGE'S UNIQUE WORKING BALANCE	
MY SPENDING PLAN	
EMBRACING MOTHERHOOD AND HOMEMAKING	
ROLE DELEGATION	
BEING A CAPTAIN OF MY SHIP	
PARENTING PARTNERSHIP	

LOVE

8. Giving Love

Love

8. Giving Love

Be like the rose in giving love: she knows which love-hooks to use to conquer hearts.

Recommended Reading Point: The Four Traits of a Cherished Muslimah: Chapter 6 - Giving Love

Giving love to others is all about finding out how they want to be loved, and giving them that. Isn't that what we want for ourselves? For our loved ones to love us the way that we want to be loved?

We can love others purposefully, emulating the Messenger of Allah ﷺ when he said:

None of you (truly) believes until he wishes for his brother what he wishes for himself.

Bukhari (13)

This habit looks at how to love your husband in the ways that he prefers to be loved, and how to use admiration and seduction to draw him towards you...

The Divine Names for Giving Love

When you cultivate the habit of giving love to others by connecting to Allah through His names, you strive to be merciful and giving, thinking of what others need and giving it to them before they ask. You strive to love unconditionally, and you do the very best you can, being enriched through His giving and mercy. You love others readily as you are quick to forgive and quick to love. When establishing the habit of giving love, connect to Allah through His names of love and generosity, by putting them into practice/submitting to them, and call upon Him with them when you pray to Him.

GIVING LOVE	
ALLAH (1)	The one who unites all the attributes of divinity
AL-MUSAWWIR (14)	The fashioner
AL-WAHĀB (17)	The bestower of gifts
ASH-SHAKŪR (36)	He who gives more than one deserves
AL-KARĪM (43)	He who gives before you ask
AL-WADŪD (48)	He who loves unconditionally
AL-MAJĪD (49)	The one who is all glorious, noble, beautiful, bountiful in His actions
AL-MUBDI (59)	The one who starts things
AL-BARR (79)	He who promises to do good to those who cherish Him
AT-TAWWĀB (80)	He who reminds you to repent and forgives you
AL-MUGHNĪ (89)	He who enriches you
AN-NĀFI (92)	The one who benefits
AR RASHID (98)	He who does the best

Exercise 8.1 Find Out How He Likes to be Loved

In order to be loved, we must first become lovers.

Harville Hendrix, Getting the Love You Want

This exercise will help you to cultivate a habit of giving love to your spouse in the ways he appreciates best. Ask your husband which of the five love languages (mentioned in Exercise 3.4) make him feel loved. Ask him to tell you in order of preference. Ask him to tell you which one he isn't really bothered about, and see if this corresponds to your own natural way of giving love. Are they the same or different?

THE LOVE LANGUAGE I USE TO SHOW MY LOVE TO HIM	THE LOVE LANGUAGE HE WANTS ME TO USE
(Let him know this is a way of expressing your love)	(Give him more of)
e.g. Quality time: we work out together	*e.g. Physical touch: giving him a neck massage*

THIS LOVE LANGUAGE IS NOT THAT IMPORTANT TO HIM

(If you currently show him love in this language, let him know this. If possible, consciously give him less of this language, freeing up your energy to give him the love he wants.)

e.g. Acts of service: keeping the house immaculate

The Four Traits of a Cherished Muslimah Workbook

Exercise 8.2 Admiration

Recommended Reading Point: The Four Traits of a Cherished Muslimah: Admiration (page 116)

Think of all the things you admire about your husband and in the following table write them down. See the examples in *The Four Traits of a Cherished Muslimah* for more ideas.

Seeking out things to admire in your spouse

APPEARANCE	*e.g. Beautiful hands*
CHARACTER	*e.g. Kind-hearted and hard-working*
TALENTS	*e.g. Great at DIY*
ACCOMPLISHMENTS	*e.g. Works hard to provide a wonderful home for me and our boys*
VALUES & BELIEFS	*e.g. Strong parenting values for our kids*
IDENTITY	*e.g. A father before anything else*

Exercise 8.3 Seduction

Recommended Reading Point: The Four Traits of a Cherished Muslimah: Physical Intimacy - Chapter 7

We have explored many ways that we can give love to our husbands. Reflect below on the ways that you could give your husband more intimate love: perhaps through looking good, dressing up, being available, or seduction—or all of them! Some examples are given below; add your own to them:

LOOK	*Wear something gorgeous, wear make-up (tastefully), light candles in the bedroom, draw attention to your neck, ears, arms… bust, bum (in private!)*
SOUND	*Compliment, appreciate, admire, express your desires…*
FEEL	*Wear something silky in bed, use massage oil, kiss him, touch him, smile at him coyly, let your body brush lightly against his when you walk past him…*
TASTE	*Chocolates, strawberries, grapes, grape juice in crystal goblets…*
SMELL	*Perfume your pulse points, perfume your pillows, light sensually scented candles, use/diffuse sensual aromatherapy oils…*

Exercise 8.4 Prayerful Loving

In this chapter, you have been establishing a habit of giving love. Looking at the love languages, you have identified your husband's love languages so that you can love him in the ways that he prefers. You have reflected on the ways that you can admire and seduce him. Revisit all of your intentions and goals for this habit and turn them into prayers, knowing that He is the most loving and has given both men and women admirable qualities. If you find any areas challenging, here is your opportunity to articulate that to Allah, asking Him for help through His beautiful and loving names.

GOALS & INTENTIONS	MY PRAYERS
MY HUSBAND'S LOVE LANGUAGES	
ADMIRATION	
SEDUCTION	

WISDOM

9. Healing
10. Time

Wisdom

9. Healing

Be like the iris in healing:
allow every petal to tell its own unique story and lesson.

Recommended Reading Point: The Four Traits of a Cherished Muslimah:
Chapter 9 – Healing

Prayerfully cultivating the habit to heal will allow you to move forward with health and vitality, without being bogged down with the weight of the past. To cultivate this habit, take stock of your supporting resources, bring your traits back into balance and look at the wounds that affect you and your husband. And then, in true Cherished Muslimah fashion, pray for it! Ask Allah to heal you. Send salawat on the Messenger of Allah ﷺ, who is the remedy of hearts and a cure for all illnesses.

O Allah, bless our Master Muhammad
the remedy of hearts and their medicine,
the cure of bodies and their health,
the light of eyes and their radiance,
And his family and companions and give them peace.

Salawat Al-Tibbiya

The Divine Names for Healing

When you cultivate the habit of healing by connecting to Allah through His names, you acknowledge that He is the one who breaks you only because He wants to make you. In His generosity, He is always bestowing gifts, even through times of hardship. He is the one who raises you and gives you honour even when you feel low. You know that Allah is the one who continually and completely forgives you each time you turn back to Him, and who loves you unconditionally, ever watchful over you and finding you whenever you are lost. You know that He is always standing for you, protecting you. With Allah, the healer, by your side, you are safe to heal. When establishing the habit of healing, connect to Allah through His names of mercy, healing and enrichment, by putting them into practice/submitting to them, and call upon Him with them when you pray to Him.

	HEALING
ALLAH (1)	The one who unites all the attributes of divinity
AR-RAHMĀN (2)	The merciful, without comparison
AR-RAHĪM (3)	The always merciful
AL-JABBĀR (10)	The maker and breaker
AL-GHAFĀR (15)	Forgives again and again
AL-WADŪD (48)	He who loves unconditionally
AL-MUBDI (59)	The one who starts things
AL-MUĪ'D (60)	The one who brings things back
AL-MUHYI (61)	The giver of life
AL-WĀJID (65)	The finder, He finds you when you are lost
AR-RAŪF (83)	The pinnacle of mercy to all
AL-MUGHNĪ (89)	He who enriches you
AN-NĀFI (92)	The one who benefits

My Supporting Resources

Only a few of My slaves are grateful.

Saba (34:13)

When going through tough times, it is easy to fall into despair and to feel alone and unsupported, yet when we focus on all the resources we have, we shift from a place of lack to abundance. In Byron Katie's book *I Need Your Love, Is That True?* she describes how everything supports us, from our neck to the chair we are sat on; from the earth we live on, to the planets that hold it in its orbit; from the man outside walking his dog to the countless number of people working behind the scenes supporting our existence: from the postman to the lady sat in the council office in charge of the street lighting. SubhanAllah!

Allah supports us and sends support to us in more ways than we will ever know. But the least we can do is to acknowledge Him for the support that we *are* aware of! A good way to become aware of His support is to get to know Him through His names. How easy is it is to forget or overlook our blessings, to forget Ar-Razzāq and Ash-Shakūr, the Abundant Giver of these blessings! How sad it is that we forget Al-Walī and Al-Wakīl, the one who is always there for us, representing us? Allah has told us that only a few of His slaves are truly grateful—so be of the few!

In the following exercise, reflect on all the resources you have in your life that support you in times of need. Which skills and capabilities has Allah blessed you with? Which values and beliefs has He instilled in you, that drive you? Which material possessions has He bestowed upon you that help you? It may be something as simple as a hot water bottle or a food processor, or it could be your back garden or even your bathtub! Which people in your life have been sent to support you? It could be a teacher or friend; a coach or counsellor; your hairdresser or even your osteopath. The people who support us may be those in our lives at this current moment, those whose company we have had the pleasure of in the past, and perhaps even those who will come in the future! I have often been driven to make changes in my life so that the females that will be born in my family and society will have better-empowered lives due to the change I strive for today. By doing this, my future daughters also become my support—how beautiful and nourishing is that feeling! Similarly, your support may come from the past; those who have lived before us, struggled for us and paved the way for us to be where we are today.

Glad tidings for us, Oh Assembly of Muslims!
When Allah named the one who called us to obey Him, 'The Noblest of Messengers'
Henceforth we become the noblest of peoples.

Imam Sharaf ad-Din al-Busiri

My number one support is the Messenger of Allah ﷺ who gave us his beautiful example and touched the lives of many who remain an inspiration until this day: the beloved people of his house, his pure wives, his noble companions and all those who followed his way, may Allah send His peace and blessings upon them all!

The Four Traits of a Cherished Muslimah Workbook

Exercise 9.1 My Supporting Resources

Supporting resources can come in many forms: knowledge, books, podcasts, home-help, grocery deliveries, parks, beaches! They can be anywhere and everywhere—what supports you?

SKILLS AND CAPABILITIES *e.g. I am diplomatic, I think before I speak*	
VALUES AND BELIEFS *e.g. I value self-improvement, I believe women are equal to men*	
MATERIAL POSSESSIONS *e.g. Aromatherapy oils, money for counselling*	
PEOPLE IN YOUR LIFE (PAST, PRESENT AND FUTURE) *e.g. My teachers, my late grandmother, the Messenger of Allah ﷺ*	
OTHER *e.g. Knowledge, books, podcasts, home-help, grocery deliveries, parks, beaches, etc.*	

Exercise 9.2 Why Won't the Gate Shut?

There was a time when my husband and I decided to clear our front garden and plant flowers in the beds. As we started clearing the weeds, we noticed one with a root that had grown so thick that it needed to be dug out with a spade. Eventually, we realised its strong, solid root was trailing through the whole of the flower bed, and as we followed it with the spade, we were shocked to realise that it was growing all the way underneath our house! We knew at that point that we needed to call a professional to help us to deal with it, as it was too deeply embedded in the foundation of our garden.

Sometimes our lives out like that—with deeply embedded issues that need to be dealt with. We can try to clear those issues by ourselves, but don't ever hesitate to get help if you feel you can't do it alone. Alhamdulillah, I feel blessed that Allah granted me the ability to be proactive to keep searching for people to help me. Whenever I have felt I can't clear a part of my emotional garden myself, I have always sought out someone who can help me. Sometimes it has been a counsellor, sometimes a coach, or simply a trusted friend.

Consider which areas of your garden need to be cleared in order for it to flourish. What do you need to change for the better? Do you need help from others to do this?

Exercise 9.3 Balance Your Excessive or Deficient Habits

*You should not be extremists but try to be near to perfection
and receive the good tidings that you will be rewarded.*

Bukhari (39)

We are often excessive or deficient in one of our four traits due to a need to be balanced in those areas. In each of the following tables, the middle column shows how to repair any imbalances for each of the twelve habits. Reflect on what you need to do to be more balanced.

Balancing excesses and deficiencies in Leadership

EXCESSIVENESS	BALANCE	DEFICIENCY
All actions and striving are to attain an outcome	**ACTIONS CONNECT TO PURPOSE**	Unable to strive as the goal seems unattainable
Hyper-focusing on certain areas and ignoring the rest	**BALANCED LIFE IN ALL AREAS**	Neglecting responsibilities due to overwhelm
Obsessing and controlling over one's charges	**EMBRACE ROLES OF GUARDIANSHIP**	Neglect and lack of control of one's charges

Balancing excesses and deficiencies in Love

EXCESSIVENESS	BALANCE	DEFICIENCY
Unappreciative of many blessings one has	**SHOW GRATITUDE FOR WHAT YOU HAVE**	Feeling unworthy of having any blessings
Too much self-care	**EXERCISE HEALTHY SELF-CARE**	Not enough self-care
Giving too much love	**GIVE HEALTHY LOVE**	Not having any love to give

Balancing excesses and deficiencies in Wisdom

EXCESSIVENESS	BALANCE	DEFICIENCY
Communicate for personal benefit	**COMMUNICATE WISELY**	Unable to communicate to one's detriment
Stubborn refusal to heal	**HEAL YOUR WOUNDS**	Perceived inability to heal
Wanting results immediately	**ALLOW TIME TO RUN ITS COURSE**	Unable to make changes to the current situation

Balancing excesses and deficiencies in Justice

EXCESSIVENESS	BALANCE	DEFICIENCY
Controlling others' lives	**RESPECTING OTHERS**	Being controlled by others
Putting own needs and wants above everyone else's	**RESPECTING YOURSELF**	Prioritising the needs of others to one's own detriment
Doing too much	**EXERCISE SELF-DISCIPLINE**	Doing too little

Acknowledging Wounds

If a wound has touched you, be sure a similar wound has touched others.

Al-Nisa (3:140)

Sometimes we need professional counselling to help us with our wounds. Who we are as people directly affects all those around us, especially our spouse and children. Josh Shipp in his book, *The Grown-Up's Guide to Teenage Humans,* found that the majority of effective, caring adults all share this particular mindset: 'You'll want and need help'. If you have identified that you have wounds which prevent you from being your best self in your relationship, seek help for it. We live in a time where we have easy access to coaches, counsellors and therapists who can help us. Admitting that we are limited in our human-ness and could use some help is an act of humility. Seeking out that help takes courage. Be of the humble and brave ones who reach out for help when they need it.

So ask the people of the message if you do not know.

Al-Anbiya (21:7)

Often we feel that we are the only ones going through a particular problem, yet these problems are often shared by the majority of us. It is natural to have grown up with hang-ups from our childhoods. It is natural to over-react when we are coming from a place of hurt and bad memories. Yet the important question is: How do we move forward with those hang-ups and memories? How do we move forward if our spouse has them? If your spouse has a wound that affects you and your family, encourage him to seek help. He may or may not choose to, but the simple fact of acknowledging and supporting him in his wounds is the first step towards his healing process.

The Four Traits of a Cherished Muslimah Workbook

Exercise 9.4 Wounds

Do you or your husband have any wounds that you are aware of? Which values, beliefs, decisions or memories do either of you have that cause you to behave negatively? What do you need to overcome this? With these filters in mind, reflect on limitations your spouse has which you can be sympathetic and understanding with? To cultivate intimacy, see how you can provide a safe refuge for your spouse, where you can help him and buffer him through your strengths and support.

ME	WAYS TO GET SUPPORT	MY HUSBAND	WAYS TO SUPPORT HIM
e.g. I grew up in an abusive home and struggle to trust my husband.	e.g. Get some therapy to overcome what happened and to practice mindfulness.	e.g. My husband hates confrontation and so he doesn't speak up to address our family's needs.	e.g. Be patient when he doesn't address our family's needs but keep encouraging and reminding him to.

Exercise 9.5 Prayerful Healing

The healing habit is about balancing any excesses or deficiencies in the four traits and empathetically identifying which wounds prevent you and your husband from being your best selves. It is not easy to change. But with Allah's help and support, it is easier. Finding it hard? Tell Him that! Don't have the strength? Tell Him that! Reflect below on what you need to change, what you need to do about it, and what help you need from Allah—and then ask Him for it, calling upon Him with His healing and protecting names, knowing that He is Al-Muʿīd and can bring back the love and well-being that was once there.

GOALS & INTENTIONS	MY PRAYERS
BALANCING THE TWELVE HABITS	
HEALING MY WOUNDS	
HELPING MY HUSBAND WITH HIS WOUNDS	

10. Time

Be like the iris in time: allowing time to runs its course while she grows wherever she is planted.

Recommended Reading Point: The Four Traits of a Cherished Muslimah: Chapter 10 – Time

Establishing the habit of time means that you acknowledge the importance that time plays in your life and marriage. You see Allah's hand in all you do. We will always experience seasons of hardship; Allah has told us that He will surely test us, but has given glad tidings to the patient ones and told them that they will be receiving His blessings and mercy. So when times are tough, remember that He is As-Sabūr, making everything happen at the right time. He is Al-Latīf, the one who does everything with subtlety; gradual, pacing, everything at the right time in the right proportions.

See your marriage as fluid—coming from the past, being in the moment and sowing seeds for the future. Bide your time and wait for growth, weathering any difficult seasons with the resources you need—don't forget your brolly when it rains, and make sure you put your winter clothes away in the summer so it doesn't clutter your wardrobe!

The habit of time gives you tools to get through your life powerfully. Nothing happens without a reason or cause, and by understanding this we can move forward to the future with empowerment.

The Divine Names for Acknowledging Time

When you cultivate the habit of time by connecting to Allah through His names, you acknowledge the importance that time plays in your life; you know that He is the one that makes things happen or delays things. He is always observing, always there yet hidden, and even though it may seem like your efforts are not bringing any fruits, you know that He does everything at the right time. When establishing the habit of time, connect to Allah through His names of divine knowledge and wisdom, by putting them into practice/submitting to them, and call upon Him with them when you pray to Him.

	TIME
ALLAH (1)	The one who unites all the attributes of divinity
AL-ALĪM (20)	He who knows everything
AS SAMĪ (27)	The all-hearing
AL-BASĪR (28)	The all-seeing
AR-RAQĪB (44)	He who is observing at all times
AL-MUJĪB (45)	The answerer of all prayers
AL-MUHSĪ (58)	He who knows the number, doesn't forget, reckons everything
AL-MUBDI (59)	The one who starts things
AL-MUQADDIM (71)	He who makes things happen, promotes them
AL-MU'AKHIR (72)	He who delays things, pushes them away
AL-AWWAL (73)	The first
AL-ĀKHIR (74)	The last
AS-SABŪR (99)	He who does everything at the right time

The Four Traits of a Cherished Muslimah Workbook

Exercise 10.1 Rainbow Results

When you shine sunbeams on raindrops, you get a rainbow.

Dee Shipman & Paul Jacobs – New Oceans NLP

Rainbows are the beautiful results of all of our raindrops (seemingly negative experiences) with all of our sunbeams (or resources) shone on them. The wise woman chases rainbows—in fact, 'iris' is the Greek word for rainbow. She wisely picks up the gifts that her past leaves behind, taking the skills and life lessons from times of hardship, and utilises them to enrich her life.

Reflect below on a time when you went through some difficulties, and your previous experiences helped you get through it. These are rainbow results. Or, think of the difficult experiences that you have had, which sunbeam resources you gained from those events, and how those resources helped you later on in your life. These are also rainbow results.

RAINDROPS	**SUNBEAMS**	**RAINBOW RESULTS**
A difficult experience that you had	Which experiences from the past helped you through it	How did resources from the past help you get through the difficult experience?
Your friend's child has an allergic reaction to nuts	*Your own child has a nut allergy so you know what to do*	*While other family members are panicking, you keep everyone calm, call an ambulance, give the child some medicine*
A difficult experience that you had	What valuable lesson you learnt from it	How that lesson helped you in the future
Grew up with a difficult father	*The importance of being a merciful parent*	*Having a merciful relationship with my child*

Exercise 10.2 Finding the Value In The Past

Sometimes He gives while depriving you [...] the deprivation becomes the same as the gift

---
Hikam - Ibn Ata illah (8384)

Understanding that Allah is the one who both protects your welfare and is the sender of all misfortune can help you to embrace a troubled past and see the gifts that you received during that difficult time, reflecting upon Allah's assurance that *'Verily, in every hardship is relief'* (94:5).

These gifts can sometimes be in the form of beneficial results of the difficult situation, or beneficial experience and skills gained during that troubled time.

The passing of time gives us experience and cultivating the habit of acknowledging the importance of time will nourish your life. With the aphorism by Ibn Ata illah in mind, reflect here on how you can learn from past negative events that you are holding on to and finding hard to let go of. They could also be negative beliefs that you have, or decisions that you made. A negative belief could be *'I'm no good at cooking'*. A negative memory/event could be *'My dad was never there when I was growing up'*. A negative decision could be *'I'm never going to invite my sister over on Eid again'*.

Ask yourself what is important about those events? What do you value now that those events have occurred? Take some time out to reflect on this exercise.

NEGATIVE EXPERIENCE THAT I'M HOLDING ON TO/KEEP REMEMBERING (BELIEFS/MEMORIES/DECISIONS)	WHAT IS IMPORTANT ABOUT HOLDING ON TO IT?	LET GO OF THE NEGATIVE EXPERIENCE, AND TAKE THE VALUE FROM IT
e.g. When I saw my sister being abused	*Taught me to protect myself*	*I release the memory, and take on the value: 'it's important to me to protect myself from harm'*
e.g. When I had a huge fall out with my family	*To make sure no one crosses my boundaries like that again*	*I release the memory, and take on the value: 'it's important to me to maintain my boundaries'*

Sowing Seeds for the Future

Once whilst I was at Centerparcs with my family, I found the perfect plaque which I now have hanging on my kitchen wall. It reads 'sow – weed – water – wait' and I think it is the perfect metaphor for life. We sow the seeds of change in our lives, keep clearing any weeds that crop up, water the seeds with nourishment, and wait for growth to take place. By Allah's permission, the sun rises every morning, and by His command, the clouds open their rain upon the land, creating beautiful growth... and rainbows to marvel and enjoy. We don't choose what grows and how—He does. He is Al-Musawwir, the beautiful fashioner and artist colouring the canvas of our lives! He decides which drop of rain is the cause of growth in our lives. Perhaps something will grow from your sowing, weeding and watering; perhaps it won't. Perhaps something will grow and you won't see the results, but your future progeny will. But... if you don't sow, nothing will grow.

The parable of my ummah is that of rain; it is not known if its beginning is better or its end.

Tirmidhi (2869)

The following worksheet will help you sow seeds of change: showing you how to weed the earth around them, nourishing them with water and sunbeams, and waiting prayerfully for the colourful growth. On the following page:

1. OUTCOME - Reflect on what outcome you would like. It's a bit like envisioning your future garden. Remember, state it in the positive as the mind doesn't recognise negatives. If I told you *not* to think of a pink elephant in a yellow-spotted dress, you would still think of one, even though I told you specifically not to!

2. SOW - Think of the steps you will need to take to achieve your outcome. Which seeds of change do you need to plant?

3. WEED – Which obstacles will you need to overcome to achieve your goal?

4. WATER – Reflect on which resources you have to achieve your desired outcome—these could be experiences, skills, values, beliefs, sources of strength (material possessions, people in your life, or more).

5. EFFECTS - What effects will this outcome have on you and those around you? Which sunbeams will come from it? Which potential raindrops may result—remembering, of course, that those difficulties are not a bad thing?

6. WAIT – You do your bit and you do your best. And then wait, prayerfully, for your garden to flourish according to Allah's decree and plan. As you wait, enjoy the rainbow and enjoy the growth.

Exercise 10.3 Sowing Seeds for the Future

OUTCOME - What do you want?

SOWING SEEDS - What steps do you have to take to get it?

REMOVING THE WEEDS – Which obstacles do you need to overcome to get it?

WATER - Which resources do you have to achieve your desired outcome? Which sunbeams do you have to shine on your raindrops?

EFFECTS - What effects will it have on you? What does your future look like when you have achieved your outcome?

WAIT – Take the steps towards creating the outcome you want. Look to see how you can overcome your obstacles, bring your resources in to help you, and then wait prayerfully. Call upon Allah, Ar-Rashīd, to do the best for you, while you do your best.

The Four Traits of a Cherished Muslimah Workbook

Exercise 10.4 Ask my Daughter

Recommended Reading Point: The Four Traits of a Cherished Muslimah: Ask My Daughter (page 192)

As described in *The Four Traits of a Cherished Muslimah,* picture/imagine yourself 25 years from now, and your daughter (real or imaginary) has come to ask you for advice for the same problems you are experiencing. How would you answer her? This exercise is different from thinking 'What advice would I give a friend?' When we connect it to one's own daughter, a female like ourselves who we would have/have such a tender and merciful bond with, we connect it to a relationship of love and compassion.

Reflect on how you would answer your daughter and what lessons you can take from your advice to her.

Exercise 10.5 Are My Marital Roots Strong Enough?

Recommended Reading Point: The Four Traits of a Cherished Muslimah: Understanding Family Roots (page 194)

If you have challenges with your in-laws, check to see if your marital roots are strong. The deeper and more established that your relationship becomes, the better you and your husband can work together to resolve the issues which commonly arise when living with or around extended family. In the cases where they need strengthening, see which of the twelve habits you need to cultivate in order to become stronger as a couple to overcome *all* the challenges of life, not just in-law struggles.

WHERE MY MARITAL ROOTS ARE WEAK	WITH WHICH HABITS CAN I STRENGTHEN MY ROOTS?		
e.g. My husband prioritises extended family get-togethers over family time	*e.g. Guardianship – making the home a place of tranquillity. Communication – expressing desires and feelings*		

Exercise 10.6 Prayerful Time

Understanding time is one of the wisest habits to cultivate in your marriage because your marriage is like a tree, and all trees are a testimony of time. They show their strength in their trunks. They start off small and weak and need protection, and end up big and powerful, scattering their fruit around them.

To establish a 'time habit', you have looked at finding value in the past and sowing seeds for the future, looking at how strong your roots are now and what you can do to make them stronger. Revisit all of your intentions and goals for this habit and turn them into prayers, invoking Allah by His names of care and wisdom.

GOALS & INTENTIONS	MY PRAYERS
FINDING VALUE IN THE PAST	
SOWING SEEDS	
ASK MY DAUGHTER	
ARE MY ROOTS STRONG ENOUGH?	

JUSTICE

11. Self-Respect
12. Self-Discipline

Justice

11. Self-Respect

Be like the gladiolus in self-respect:
her swords ensure that she is safe to grow and flourish.

Recommended Reading Point: The Four Traits of a Cherished Muslimah:
Chapter 12 – Self-Respect

The habit of self-respect ensures that you have fences in your garden to keep the good stuff in and the bad stuff out. Self-respect means you cultivate the skills to remain centred and connected when establishing boundaries—it's no good if you fly off the handle each time you want to establish a new boundary. Upholding self-respect means you eliminate the things that harm your marriage. Chapter 13 of *The Four Traits of a Cherished Muslimah* looks at a few common toxic influences in marriages and how you can deal with them. Boundaries ultimately distinguish you from your husband as being together yet separate, where both of you can flourish in your own spaces, together.

The Divine Names for Self-Respect

When you cultivate the habit of self-respect by connecting to Allah through His names, you acknowledge that Allah is elevated above all. He is the giver and taker of honour. He is the ultimate judge and through this knowledge, you try to ensure that others treat you according to His laws. You are secure in knowing that He will stand for you and take responsibility for you, and even though you strive to uphold your rights, you never take revenge for yourself but ensure that justice is upheld at all times. When establishing the habit of self-respect, connect to Allah through His names of justice and power, by putting them into practice/submitting to them, and call upon Him with them when you pray to Him.

SELF-RESPECT	
ALLAH (1)	The one who unites all the attributes of divinity
AL-JABBĀR (10)	The maker and breaker
AL-QAHĀR (16)	The oppressor, dominator of enemies
AL-MU'IZ (25)	The giver of honour
AL-ADL (30)	He who is just in rulings and proportions
AL-HAFĪDH (39)	The preserver and protector
AL-WAKĪL (53)	He who takes responsibility for you
AL-QAWĪ (54)	The strong, perfect power
AL-MATĪN (55)	The firm, intensified strength
AL-WALĪ (56)	He who will stand for the believer
AL-MUNTAQIM (81)	He who doesn't take revenge for himself
AL-MUQSIT (86)	The just in equity and fairness
AL-MĀNI (90)	The protector, creates causes for protection, the powerful withholder

Here's a list of the areas where we need boundaries, as explained in Chapter 12 of *The Four Traits of a Cherished Muslimah*:

1. House
2. Body
3. Marriage
4. Children
5. Family
6. Time
7. Religion
8. Identity
9. Finances

This part of the workbook is about respecting yourself through establishing healthy boundaries if you haven't got them already. A word of warning, though! If you are in a situation where you are lacking boundaries in *many* of the above areas, you may need coaching or counselling to help you through this. Also, try not to apply too many boundaries all at once; pace yourself or you may be in danger of becoming a boundary junkie. Be careful that in your attempt to put fences around your garden, you don't seal yourself into a high-walled prison! It would be wise to differentiate between the big stuff and the small stuff and work on dealing with the big stuff first.

The gladiolus has the perfect balance of love and self-protection. Notice her sword-like leaves and upward growing flowers, symbolising her strength and fierceness. Yet her beautiful flowers show us that boundaries don't necessarily need to be ugly or unpleasant. When we have loving boundaries, we are still loving and beautiful, whilst simultaneously being firm and safe.

On the following page, identify the areas in which you are lacking boundaries. Note which of these areas you would class as 'big stuff', and reflect on how you would establish your boundaries, and how you would communicate these boundaries and limits to your spouse. We can remind others of our boundaries, again and again, knowing that At-Tawwāb does the same with us: He forgives us repeatedly when we slip and make a mistake.

The Four Traits of a Cherished Muslimah Workbook

Exercise 11.1 Boundaries – Big and Small

	BIG/SMALL	COMMUNICATE I WANT/I DON'T WANT/I CAN'T/I FEEL/I NEED
1. House – safety and privacy		
2. Body – health care and safety		
3. Marriage – intimacy/porn/polygamy		
4. Kids – parenting partnership		
5. Time - balanced		
6. Family & in-laws		
7. Religion – freedom to practise		
8. Identity – freedom to own life and opinions		
9. Dreams – freedom to own desires and wishes		
10. Finances – your own and from your husband		

Exercise 11.2 Crash vs Coach

C	CONTRACTION	Contract in defence	**C**	CENTRED	Centre and remind yourself what is important to you and your husband
R	REACTION	React to what was said	**O**	OPEN	Open your heart so you can be your best self, open your mind so you are aware of different points of view
A	ANALYSIS	Begin to analyse and hyper-focus on problems	**A**	AWARE	Be aware of your needs and also the needs of others
S	SEPARATION	Separate from husband who is causing us grief	**C**	CONNECTION	Stay connected to Allah, His Messenger ﷺ, your resources and all the good your husband has
H	HURT	Hurting and hating, crash	**H**	HOLDING	Hold what emerges from the interaction, focus on all positive outcomes, and hold the negative outcomes too

Reflect on how you can use the COACH model to stay grounded in a moment of potential conflict:

C	O	A	C	H
Centre on what's important to you & your spouse	**Open** your heart & mind	**(Be) Aware** of your needs & his	**Connect** to Allah & His Messenger and to all the good within you and your husband	**Hold** all positive outcomes and the negative ones, too

Exercise 11.3 Parasites in Your Marriage

In the film *Fireproof,* a Christian man saves his marriage which is on the brink of divorce, by following a forty-day procedure based on a self-help book called 'The Love Dare'. On one of the days, the task is to eradicate parasites in the couple's lives. In the film, we see that the man's parasite is pornography, which damages his soul and his intimate relationship with his wife. Similarly, the woman has parasites too: she has friends who speak badly of their husbands, mocking and belittling them.

This exercise is about identifying and removing the parasites in your marriage. A parasite is anything that latches on to you or your partner and sucks the life out of your relationship. They are usually in the form of:

- Addictions
- Well-meaning family or friends
- The well-meaning 'inner voice'
- Comparing our husbands to other men

They promise pleasure and/or comfort but grow like a disease and consume more and more of your thoughts, time, money and energy. They steal away the loyalty of your heart from those you love. Marriages rarely survive if parasites are present. If you love your partner, you must rid yourself of any parasites in your marriage. If you don't, they will destroy you.

Our menfolk are particularly susceptible to addictions such as pornography, due to their visual nature. However, women can often have just as dangerous parasites present, in the form of well-meaning friends who offer destructive advice with the very best of intentions, negative thought patterns which destroy the quality of our life, and other men who we use as a shining example (privately or even aloud). Any one of these parasites will chip away at your marriage. I'm not saying that they are all the same in their gravity, however; viewing pornography is a far more serious parasite than a gossiping friend, for instance.

Our negative thought patterns often stem from a very good intention, and it may have been very important for us at the time we developed that thought and idea, yet that pattern may not be as effective today.

Do you have any parasites present in your marriage? Make a list of them here:

Exercise 11.4 Separateness

In which areas do you have different values to your husband? Reflect on these areas, and how you can take the initiative to live these values. Also, reflect on the values your husband has that differ to yours, and in which ways you can support him in living them. How can these values help to bring strength and skills into your marriage's unique working balance?

ME	US	HIM
Taking the initiative to live these values	**Joint partnership**	**Supporting him to live his values**
When we have different values	When we are in harmony with our opinions	When we have different values
e.g. To go to the gym twice a week	*e.g. To encourage our children to pray their salah*	*e.g. To go to weekly dhikr gatherings*

Exercise 11.5 I'm Okay, You're Okay

When setting boundaries in your marriage, it is important to see if these boundaries create win-win situations for both you and your spouse. It is ineffective for one spouse to get the benefits from the application of boundaries, and for the other spouse to be suffering. If this happens, the attempt to set boundaries will often lead to conflict.

No one likes to have boundaries imposed on them, and it is common to face resistance, so check to see if you are being fair and taking your spouse's needs and desires into consideration as well as your own.

Compromises don't have to be totally equal but they give hope and room for further discussion.

Nancy Wasserman Cocola – Six in the Bed

Reflect on how effective your boundary setting is using the following table:

	YOU'RE OKAY	YOU'RE NOT OKAY
I'M OKAY	*The biscuit cupboard contains biscuits we both like.*	*We only buy biscuits that I like.*
I'M NOT OKAY	*We only buy biscuits that you like.*	*There are no biscuits in the biscuit cupboard.*

Exercise 11.6 Moving On: Should I or Shouldn't I?

Moving on is a very difficult and personal decision. There is often no right or wrong answer, and the following exercise in Cartesian Doubt[7] helps explore the different possibilities that would (or wouldn't) arise if you moved on (or didn't).

WHAT WOULD HAPPEN IF I DID?	WHAT WOULD HAPPEN IF I DIDN'T?
WHAT WOULDN'T HAPPEN IF I DID?	**WHAT WOULDN'T HAPPEN IF I DIDN'T?**

Exercise 11.7 Prayerful Self-Respect

This chapter is one of the largest chapters in *The Four Traits of a Cherished Muslimah*, as the self-respect habit is often misunderstood. To cultivate this habit, you have looked at which boundaries need to be established (to avoid becoming a boundary 'junkie') and differentiated between your needs and desires, taking the necessary steps to get your needs met. This habit looks at staying grounded during times of conflict, eliminating 'parasites' and keeping your own identity in your marriage while simultaneously working on win-win solutions. Revisit all of your intentions and goals for this habit and turn them into prayers, knowing that Allah is your representative and Al-Wakīl.

GOALS & INTENTIONS	MY PRAYERS
BOUNDARIES – BIG AND SMALL	
WANTS VS NEEDS	
CRASH VS COACH	
PARASITES IN MY MARRIAGE	
SEPARATENESS	
I'M OKAY, YOU'RE OKAY	
MOVING ON?	

12. Self-Discipline

Be like the gladiolus in self-discipline:
her swords remind her to check herself from doing too much or too little.

Recommended Reading Point: The Four Traits of a Cherished Muslimah:
Chapter 14 – Self-Discipline

On pages 34–37 of *The Four Traits of a Cherished Muslimah*, you read about the negative characteristics that manifest when we are either excessive or deficient in the four traits. Cultivating the habit of self-discipline ensures that you are not a woman who does too much, nor are you a woman who does too little.

If you are excessive, reflect on the things to let go of; if you are deficient, think of things to start doing. In doing so, you can become a balanced and disciplined leader by ensuring you prioritise your life by putting first things first.

The Divine Names for Self-Discipline

When you cultivate the habit of self-discipline by connecting to Allah through His names, you acknowledge that Allah is your witness and you submit to His power, knowing that you don't have to do it all, but at the same time you must fulfil your rights to yourself and others through His power and strength. You take responsibility for where you either do too much or too little. You also know that when you do cause yourself harm, He cures you whenever you turn back to Him. When establishing the habit of self-discipline, connect to Allah through His names of justice and creation, by putting them into practice/submitting to them, and call upon Him with them when you pray to Him.

SELF-DISCIPLINE	
ALLAH (1)	The one who unites all the attributes of divinity
AL-ADL (30)	He who is just in rulings and proportions
AL-HASĪB (41)	He who takes account, the sufficiency (when needs not met)
AL-BĀ'ITH (50)	He who brings forth something out of nothing
AL-MUBDI (59)	The one who starts things
AL-MUĪ'D (60)	The one who brings things back
AL-WĀJID (65)	The finder, He finds you when you are lost
AL-WĀLI (77)	He who takes responsibility over everything
AL-MUQSIT (86)	The just in equity and fairness
AL-JĀMI (87)	The gatherer, uniter, combines similar, dissimilar, opposites
AD-DĀR (91)	The one who harms
AN-NĀFI (92)	The one who benefits
AR-RASHĪD (98)	He who does the best

Exercise 12.1 Being a Balanced Leader

*And the forerunners, the forerunners –
Those are the ones brought near [to Allah]
in the gardens of pleasure.*

Al-Waq'ia (56:7–12)

It's time to develop the habit of self-discipline! If you are a woman who does too much, reflect on which areas of your life you are doing too much in, and what would happen if you let go of those responsibilities, perhaps delegated them to someone else, or perhaps eliminated in your life? What sort of effect would it have on you, and what effect would it have on your marriage?

If you are a woman who does too little, reflect on the things you can start doing or take responsibility of. You can create a home by picking up your baton and partaking in the race to be one of the forerunners!

THINGS TO LET GO OF/ START DOING	THE EFFECT IT WILL HAVE ON ME	THE EFFECT IT WILL HAVE ON MY MARRIAGE
e.g. Letting go of having a perfect house.	*I will feel more relaxed.*	*If I am relaxed, it will make our marriage happier.*
e.g. Start having meals together as a family.	*I will be glad to have everyone together.*	*It will create a happier home.*

Exercise 12.2 Living in the Shadows of Leadership

Reflect here on what happens when a woman is excessive in her leadership trait and when she is deficient in her leadership trait. What effects does it have on her family, and how can she balance it successfully?

CHARACTERISTICS OF A WOMAN WHO IS EXCESSIVE IN HER LEADERSHIP TRAIT	CHARACTERISTICS OF A WOMAN WHO IS DEFICIENT IN HER LEADERSHIP TRAIT
HOW IT AFFECTS HER AND HER FAMILY	**HOW IT AFFECTS HER AND HER FAMILY**
I HAVE A TENDENCY TO BE EXCESSIVE/ DEFICIENT IN MY LEADERSHIP TRAIT	**IT WOULD HELP IF I WAS MORE….**

First Things First – Time Quadrant

Complementary healing therapist Zuhair Girach explains that just as there are twenty-four hours in a day and once those hours are finished, there's no way of getting any more, we similarly have an allotted amount of energy each day, and once it's all used up, we won't have any more left. Therefore, we have to be very careful where we direct our energy. If we spend it on the not-so-important things, we won't have anything left to expend on the important things.

This is Stephen Covey's Time Quadrant. It helps us to differentiate between *what's important and what's not,* and between *what's urgent and what's not.* The aim is to spend most of one's time in the Not Urgent & Important quadrant and to eliminate time spent in the Not Urgent & Not Important quadrant. Women who do too much spend a lot of time in the Urgent & Not Important quadrant, whereas women who do too little spend a lot of time in the Not Urgent & Not Important quadrant.

If we direct the majority of it to things that drain us, it is likely that we won't have the energy to live a life of quality and value. See what you can eliminate or leave out to live in the Not Urgent & Important quadrant, as that's where you ideally want to spend most of your time and energy.

The Four Traits of a Cherished Muslimah Workbook

Exercise 12.3 First Things First – Time Quadrant

URGENT & IMPORTANT	NOT URGENT & IMPORTANT
QUADRANT OF NECESSITY	**QUADRANT OF QUALITY AND VALUE**
The strategy: do it now!	The strategy: schedule time; pace yourself
e.g. Having a flare-up in the body	e.g. Eat healthy foods

URGENT & NOT IMPORTANT	NOT URGENT & NOT IMPORTANT
QUADRANT OF DECEPTION	**QUADRANT OF WASTE**
The strategy: leave it out	The strategy: eliminate
e.g. Taking an unexpected phonecall when extremely busy	e.g. Mindlessly flicking through Facebook feed

Exercise 12.4 A Prayerful Portrait: A Garden in the Future

The beauty of your inner garden is that you get to choose what's in it. You make the decisions: it can be however big or small you want it to be, and it can be your very own design. You choose how much time, energy and money you invest in your garden. In your garden, you may not be able to control certain factors, but with tender, loving care and cultivation, you can build on it and increase its dimensions.

My garden, my life

In this final exercise, write about your garden in the future. Be as descriptive as possible. What does your garden look like? What do you look like? And once you have done that, pray for it!

MY GARDEN	ME	MY PRAYER

The Four Traits of a Cherished Muslimah Workbook

Exercise 12.5 Prayerful Self-Discipline

This chapter was about cultivating a habit of self-discipline in your life, where you looked at how you can create a loving home by either doing less if you tend to do too much or more if you tend to do too little. For women who do too much, this habit can ensure that you are disciplined enough to have enough time for your children, your husband, and more importantly, yourself. Remember, doing too much is paradoxical. In trying to do it all, you deplete your energy and are unable to do anything.

For women who do too little, this habit ensures that you embrace your leadership role, get active and reconnect with yourself. Balancing the four traits in your life is an ideal place to start! Revisit all of your intentions and goals for this habit of self-discipline and turn them into prayers, invoking Allah by His names of majesty and God-consciousness:

GOALS & INTENTIONS	MY PRAYERS
I AM A WOMAN WHO DOES TOO MUCH	
SIMPLIFY MOTHERHOOD	
FREE UP TIME FOR MY HUSBAND	
FREE UP TIME FOR MYSELF	
BE A CALMER MUM	
SUPPORT MY HUSBAND BY CREATING A HOME	
I AM A WOMAN WHO DOES TOO LITTLE	
EMBRACE MY LEADERSHIP ROLE	
GET ACTIVE	
RECONNECT WITH MY INTERESTS	
SOCIALISE WITH FAMILY AND FRIENDS	
COMMUNICATE EFFECTIVELY	
FIX MY LIFE, NOT OTHERS'	

Afterword

A Portrait of a Cherished Muslimah

She is the leader

A Cherished Muslimah has purpose. She acknowledges that Allah is her purpose for everything, as He created her, is the highest, the first and the last. He possesses all majesty and power and never perishes. He is the one purpose and intention...

She has balance. She acknowledges that Allah proportions everything in the perfect balance. He is the one who is merciful to all—not just a certain group. In acknowledging this, she ensures she balances the different roles in her life, including the role of giving rights to her own body. She submits to His perfect balance and His ability to bring everything together in harmony, and in doing so, strives to bring balance and harmony into her life...

She is a guardian. She ensures that she is as merciful and fair as she can be, looking after the needs and wants of those in her charge. She is innovative, creating and fashioning solutions unique for her family, giving and nourishing them within her means and abilities. She brings life to her home through His power and as He looks after all of her needs, she in turns looks after the needs of others, using her intuition to fulfil the needs of those under her care...

She is the lover

A Cherished Muslimah has gratitude. She acknowledges that it is Allah who has designed everything so perfectly for her. He is the generous, the bestower of provision and gifts. He is the one who nourishes her with all the blessings she has in her life. She realises that gratitude brings life back into relationships with others and she is ever grateful to Him. When her loved ones praise her, she thanks them and directs the praise back to Him. She shows gratitude and connects to Allah by continually forgiving those around her and being enriched through Him...

She practises self-care. She acknowledges that Allah is the most merciful, caring and loving. She submits to His perfection and focuses on looking after herself, despite her weaknesses and flaws. She admits when she needs to rest, and gives her body its rights, acknowledging all her striving and giving herself respite for it. She nourishes herself through the gifts He has given her, and constantly praises Him while she looks after herself...

She gives others love. She strives to be merciful and giving, thinking of what others need and giving it to them before they ask. She strives to love unconditionally, and she does the very best she can, being enriched through His giving and mercy. She loves others so readily as she is quick to forgive and quick to love...

She is the wise woman

A Cherished Muslimah communicates wisely. She acknowledges that Allah is the one with knowledge of all things, the all-seeing and all-hearing, knowing that He is the one who makes things happen or delays things and He takes account of everything. She reflects and ponders her situation and informs others wisely and truthfully, knowing that through Him, she will get the perfect results...

She takes the means to heal. She acknowledges that Allah is the one who will make her through her wounds. In His generosity, He is always bestowing gifts, even through times of hardship. He is the one who raises her and gives her honour even when she may feel low. She knows that Allah is the one who continually and completely forgives her each time she turns back to Him, and who loves her unconditionally, ever watchful over her and finding her whenever she is lost. She knows that He is always standing for her, protecting her. With Allah, the healer, by her side, she is safe to heal...

She acknowledges the importance that time plays in her life. She knows that He is that one that makes things happen or delays things. In His wisdom, He is the one who exposes and opens things, observing at all times, He gathers everything together to make it happen at the correct time. Even though it may seem like her efforts are not bringing any fruits, she knows that He is always there and hidden, and He does everything at the right time.

She is the warrior

A Cherished Muslimah respects others. She acknowledges that Allah is the judge, and she ensures that all of her dealings with others are all according to His law. She brings into practice His names of honour by honouring others. She knows He will stand for her, protect her and be a witness for her and so armed with this power—His power—she knows she can be respectful no matter what situation she finds herself in...

She has self-respect. She acknowledges that Allah is elevated above all. He is the giver and taker of honour. He is the ultimate judge and through this knowledge, she tries to ensure that others treat her according to His laws. She is secure in knowing that He will stand for her and take responsibility for her, and even though she strives to uphold her rights, she never takes revenge for herself but ensures that justice is upheld at all times.

She has self-discipline. She acknowledges that Allah is her witness and she submits to his power, knowing that she doesn't have to do it all, but at the same time she must fulfil her rights to herself and others through His power and strength. She takes responsibility for where she either does too much or too little. She also knows that when she does cause herself harm, He cures her whenever she turns back to Him.

In short, a Cherished Muslimah manifests the four traits while seeing, feeling and hearing through Allah. All her thoughts, words, intentions and actions are for Him and in submission of Him. And in doing this, He loves her.

Afterword

My slave continues to draw near to Me with supererogatory works so that I shall love him. When I love him, I am his hearing with which he hears, his seeing with which he sees, his hand with which he strikes and his foot with which he walks.

Were he to ask [something] of Me, I would surely give it to him and were he to ask Me for refuge, I would surely grant it to him.

I do not hesitate about anything as much as I hesitate about [seizing] the soul of My faithful slave: he hates death and I hate hurting him.

Hadith Qudsi - Bukhari (6502)

I pray that these exercises were beneficial to you. Throughout this book, you have connected with your purpose and clarified your intentions. You have evaluated and revaluated how and why you do and say things. You have connected our modern-day customs to the Messenger of Allah ﷺ, who is a perfect example and role model, and who showed us how to live a life in balance. Furthermore, you have done all of this prayerfully, connecting to Allah through His beautiful names.

We can only do our very best. We can give it 100%. And then we leave it with Allah, knowing that whatever Allah decrees for us is in our best interests and all Allah wants us to do is worship Him with our words and actions. I would like to end with an aphorism of Shaykh Ibn Ata illah al-Iskandari:

Intentions cannot pierce the walls of predestined decrees

Hikam - Ibn Ata illah (3)

Oh Allah!
Shower Your Peace and Blessings Upon
The coolness of our eyes and the joy of our souls,
Our Master Muhammad ﷺ
and his family.

A Garden with Flowers

And so, in your beautiful, floral garden...

Be like the lily

Be like the lily in her purpose: stand out, do your best and bloom when Allah wants you to

Be like the lily in balance: be in effortless harmony with other flowers, despite being the queen

Be like the lily in her guardianship: procreating and nurturing in harmony with the masculine

Be like the rose

Be like the rose in gratitude: allow your small buds to flourish with gratitude for every blessing

Be like the rose in her self-care: her thorns protect her growth and well-being

Be like the rose in giving love: she knows which love-hooks to use to conquer hearts

Be like the iris

Be like the iris in her communication: flexible and creative with her words

Be like the iris in healing: allow every petal to tell its own unique story and lesson

Be like the iris in time: allowing time to runs its course while she grows wherever she is planted

Be like the gladiolus

Be like the gladiolus when respecting others: ensuring that her (s)words don't cause anyone undue harm

Be like the gladiolus in self-respect: her swords ensure that she is safe to grow and flourish

Be like the gladiolus in self-discipline: her swords remind her to check herself from doing too much or too little

In your garden, may you be these beautiful flowers

May you be a strong and powerful tree

May your roots run deep

May your and your husband's trees grow beautifully next to each other

May your roots intertwine with each other

May you keep certain other roots separate and honour them

May your garden flourish, and may you flourish, and be a source of nourishment and comfort to all those around you.

Ameen.

The 99 Names of Allah

ALLAH (1)	The one who unites all the attributes of divinity
AR-RAHMĀN (2)	The merciful, without comparison
AR-RAHĪM (3)	The always merciful
AL-MALIK (4)	The king, ruler
AL-QUDŪS (5)	The flawless, transcends every attribute of perfection
AS-SALĀM (6)	He who is perfect, flawless, free from any insufficiency
AL-MU'MIN (7)	He who has all the knowledge about Him
AL-MUHAYMIN (8)	He who encompasses needs/wants
AL-AZĪZ (9)	The invincible, eminent: so significant, for whom there is an intense need
AL-JABBĀR (10)	The maker and breaker
AL-MUTAKABBIR (11)	He who is elevated above all
AL-KHĀLIQ (12)	The creator
AL-BĀRI (13)	The producer, without any previous example
AL-MUSAWWIR (14)	The fashioner
AL-GHAFĀR (15)	Forgives again and again
AL-QAHĀR (16)	The oppressor, dominator of enemies

AL-WAHĀB (17)	The bestower of gifts
AR-RAZZĀQ (18)	The giver, provider
AL-FATĀH (19)	The exposer/opener of truth
AL-ALĪM (20)	He who knows everything
AL-QĀBID (21)	He who takes away
AL-BĀSIT (22)	He who spreads out
AL-KHĀFID (23)	He who brings down
AR-RĀFI (24)	He who raises up
AL-MU'IZ (25)	The giver of honour
AL-MUDHIL (26)	The taker of honour
AS-SAMĪ (27)	The all-hearing
AL-BASĪR (28)	The all-seeing
AL-HAKAM (29)	The judge
AL-ADL (30)	He who is just in rulings and proportions
AL-LATĪF (31)	The subtle, He who leads one onto an unexpected path
AL-KHABĪR (32)	The one who informs to ponder and reflect
AL-HALĪM (33)	He who forgives when angry, even if one is deserving of it
AL-ADHEEM (34)	The tremendous

AL-GHAFŪR (35)	The continuously forgiving
ASH-SHAKŪR (36)	He who gives more than one deserves
AL-ALĪ (37)	The high, above Him there is no rank or status
AL-KABĪR (38)	The great, in essence and existence, without comparison
AL-HAFĪDH (39)	The preserver and protector
AL-MUQĪT (40)	The maintainer and nourisher of food and knowledge
AL-HASĪB (41)	He who takes account, the sufficiency (when needs not met)
AL-JALĪL (42)	He who is magnificent in all ways, the perfection of all attributes of majesty
AL-KARĪM (43)	He who gives before you ask
AR-RAQĪB (44)	He who is observing at all times
AL-MUJĪB (45)	The answerer of all prayers
AL-WĀSI' (46)	He who has power over everything/sees everything
AL-HAKĪM (47)	The wise
AL-WADŪD (48)	He who loves unconditionally
AL-MAJĪD (49)	The one who is all glorious, noble, beautiful, bountiful in His actions
AL-BĀ'ITH (50)	He who brings forth something out of nothing
ASH-SHAHĪD (51)	The witness
AL-HAQQ (52)	The truth

AL-WAKĪL (53)	He who takes responsibility for you
AL-QAWĪ (54)	The strong, perfect power
AL-MATĪN (55)	The firm, intensified strength
AL-WALĪ (56)	He who will stand for the believer
AL-HAMĪD (57)	He who praises Himself
AL-MUHSĪ (58)	He who knows the number, doesn't forget, reckons everything
AL-MUBDI (59)	The one who starts things
AL-MUĪ'D (60)	The one who brings things back
AL-MUHYI (61)	The giver of life
AL-MUMĪT (62)	The taker of life
AL-HAYY (63)	The living
AL-QAYYŪM (64)	The self-existing
AL-WĀJID (65)	The finder, He finds you when you are lost
AL-MĀJID (66)	Name of majesty, all glorious, noble, beautiful, bountiful, more emphatic
AL-WĀHID (67)	He who is alone, no one shares in His oneness
AL-AHAD (68)	The one
AL-QĀDIR (69)	He who has power to do anything
AL-MUQTADIR (70)	The determiner of power, emphatic of Al-Qādir

AL-MUQADDIM (71)	He who makes things happen, promotes them
AL-MU'AKHIR (72)	He who delays things, pushes them away
AL-AWWAL (73)	The first
AL-ĀKHIR (74)	The last
AD-DHĀHIR (75)	He who is always there
AL-BĀTIN (76)	He who is hidden
AL-WĀLI (77)	He who takes responsibility over everything
AL-MUTA'ĀLI (78)	He who is elevated above all, intensified of Al-Alī
AL-BARR (79)	He who promises to do good to those who cherish Him
AT-TAWWĀB (80)	He who reminds you to repent and forgives you
AL-MUNTAQIM (81)	He who doesn't take revenge for himself
AL-AFŪ' (82)	He who forgives and forgets
AR-RAŪF (83)	The pinnacle of mercy to all
AL-MĀLIK AL-MULK (84)	The possessor of all the world
DHUL JALĀL WAL-IKRĀM (85)	The possessor of majesty and generosity
AL-MUQSIT (86)	The just in equity and fairness
AL-JĀMI (87)	The gatherer, uniter, combines similar, dissimilar, opposites
AL-GHANĪ (88)	The rich, independent

AL-MUGHNĪ (89)	He who enriches you
AL-MĀNI (90)	The protector, creates causes for protection, the powerful withholder
AD-DĀR (91)	The one who harms
AN-NĀFI (92)	The one who benefits
AN-NŪR (93)	The light (of guidance)
AL-HĀDI (94)	The guide (to the light)
AL-BADĪ (95)	The absolute cause, originator
AL-BĀQI (96)	The first
AL-WĀRITH (97)	The last
AR-RASHĪD (98)	He who does the best
AS-SABŪR (99)	He who does everything at the right time

Endnotes

1. This is the basis of Transactional Analysis, a method of therapy developed by psychiatrist Eric Berne.

2. A concept explained in both *King, Warrior, Magician, Lover* by Roger Moore and Douglas Gillette, and *Love and Respect* by Emerson Eggerichs.

3. http://www.flylady.net/ The Flylady teaches people to eliminate their clutter and establish simple routines to get their homes organised. Frazzled Franny is a woman that the Flylady describes as a woman whose life and home is overcome with chaos.

4. *Don't Sweat the Small Stuff - and it's All Small Stuff* is the first in a best-selling series of self-help books written by Dr. Richard Carlson. The premise behind the series is to stop letting little things take over your life.

5. *The Five Languages of Apology*, by Dr. Gary Chapman and Jennifer Thomas.

6. Hygge (pronounced 'hue-guh') is the Danish word for 'cosy' 'special' or 'pleasureable'. Think hot cups of cocoa, comforting stews, blankets, candles and twinkle lights.

7. Cartesian Doubt is a systematic process created by René Descartes, in which one can examine one's reasoning, often bringing about realisations that one had overlooked.

Bibliography

Cocola, Nancy Wasserman, *Six in the Bed: Dealing with Parents, In-Laws and Their Impact on Your Marriage* (Perigee Books, 1997)

Covey, Stephen R., *First Things First* (Simon & Schuster Ltd, 1994)

Dobson, James, *Love Must Be Tough: New Hope for Marriages in Crisis* (Tyndale, 2010)

Doyle, Laura, *The Surrendered Wife* (Simon & Schuster Ltd, 2001)

Gray, John, *How To Get What You Want And Want What You Have: A Practical and Spiritual Guide to Personal Success* (Vermilion, 2001)

Katie, Byron, *I Need Your Love, Is That True?* (Three Rivers Press, 2006)

Moore, Robert and Gillette, Douglas, *King, Warrior, Magician, Lover* (Bravo Ltd, 1992)

al-Sakandari, Ibn Ata illah, *The Book of Wisdoms – Kitab al Hikam* (White Thread Press, 2014)

Shine, Darla, *Happy Housewives* (HarperCollins, 2009)

Shipp, Josh, *The Grown-Up's Guide to Teenage Humans* (HarperCollins, 2018)

Stadlen, Naomi, *What Mothers Do, When It Looks Like Nothing* (Piatkus, 2005)

Notes

Notes

Notes

Notes

About the author

Sara has been coaching women and couples to cultivate nourished marriages for the last decade and offers face-to-face and online coaching from her home in West London. She lives with her husband Jawad, her parents-in-law, her three grown-up sons, her young daughter whom she homeschools, and their cat. She runs online courses and weekend workshops around the UK. You can keep up-to-date with her activities at http://www.cherishedandsuccessful.com/